Nietzsche and the Nazis

A Personal View

Stephen Hicks, Ph.D.

OCKHAM'S RAZOR PUBLISHING

Nietzsche and the Nazis documentary created by N² Productions and published by Ockham's Razor Publishing in 2006. ISBN: 9492262049. ASIN: B000JMJQGS

Nietzsche and the Nazis book published by Ockham's Razor Publishing in 2010 and 2023.

Cover design, book design, and layout by Christopher Vaughan. Cover art © Christopher Vaughan, 2010

23 24 25 26 27   7 6 5 4 3 2 1

First Edition   First Paperback Printing

Library of Congress Cataloging-in-Publication Data pending

Hicks, Stephen R. C., 1960-
Nietzsche and the Nazis / Stephen Hicks.
    p.168   cm.
Includes bibliographic references. Includes index.

ISBN: 9798389749849 (Paperback)

1. Title.   2. History, German.   3. Socialism—History.   4. National Socialism.   5. Nietzsche, Friedrich (1844-1900).

This book is printed on acid-free paper.

Printed in USA.

Table of Contents

Part 1. Introduction: Philosophy and History

1. Fascinated by history

Think about why we are fascinated by history. All of those outstanding individuals and exotic peoples. The rise and fall of civilizations—and wondering why that happens. How *did* classical Greece achieve its Golden Age—the age of Socrates and Pericles, Euripides and Hippocrates? What explains the remarkable confluence of so many outstanding individuals in one era?

Why, almost two thousand years later, did the Italian Renaissance happen? Leonardo, Michelangelo, Machiavelli, Raphael—again an incredible outpouring of genius in the arts, sciences, and politics.

Jumping ahead three centuries: What made possible the Industrial Revolution and its awesome outpouring of productivity? The ancient Chinese and the ancient Romans made impressive technological advancements—but nothing on the scale of the Industrial Revolution. Why did the Industrial Revolution first take root initially in England and Scotland? Why not in Burma or Botswana?

Or what, by contrast, explains major historical declines? Why did the Roman Empire collapse? The most powerful civilization of the ancient world imploded and became defenseless before successive waves of barbarian invasion. And before the Romans, the powerful military empires of the Hittites, the Assyrians, and the Babylonians also collapsed. Is there a common pattern at work here?

Why did the French Revolution go so horribly wrong, descending in a reign of paranoia, fratricide, and terror? Why, by contrast, did the American Revolution, in many ways fighting the same kind of battle and subject to the same desperate pressures, not go the same self-destructive route? How, a century and a half later, could the most educated nation in Europe become a Nazi dictatorship?

All these questions raise issues of dramatic historical change, for better or worse. But we can also ask questions about long periods during which no dramatic changes took place. Consider the San people of the Kalahari area in Southern Africa, sometimes called Bushmen. Experts estimate that for 10,000 years the San have lived the same way for generation after generation. Let us put that in perspective. If a generation is twenty-five years or so, then 10,000 years means 400 generations of sameness. By contrast, it has been only about twenty generations since Columbus crossed the Atlantic—and consider how much has changed in Europe and the Americas since then.

Yet even the 10,000 years of the San people is dwarfed by the estimated 35,000 years that the Aborigines of Australia have existed in essentially the same way generation after generation. 35,000 years ago is approximately when Neanderthal Man was becoming extinct. Why did the cultures of the San and the Aborigines *not* change for such unimaginably long stretches of time?

2. *What is philosophy of history?*

These are fascinating questions. As historians we study interesting individuals and cultures to understand how they lived, why they lived the way they did, and what impact they had on the course of human events. As philosophers we think more broadly and abstractly. We learn our lessons from the historians and ask: Are there broader explanations we can find in the dramatic rises and falls of cultures, or in the static nature of others?

History, from this perspective, is a huge laboratory of experiments in human living. Some of those experiments have been wildly successful, some have achieved middling results, leading their cultures to eke out an existence across the generations—and some have been outright disasters, causing misery and death on a large scale. Can we identify the fundamental causes at work? Can we learn why some cultures flourish while others stagnate, collapse, or descend into horror? Is there a moral to the story of history?

Let us turn to one major experiment, one that turned out to be one of the darkest eras in human history.

Part 2. Explaining Nazism Philosophically

3. How could Nazism happen?

How could Nazism happen? This is an important question: professors and teachers the world over use the Nazis as a prime example of evil and rightly so. The Nazis were enormously destructive, killing 20 million people during their twelve-year reign. They were not the *most* destructive regime of the twentieth century: Josef Stalin and the other Communist dictators of the Soviet Union killed sixty-two million people. Mao Zedong and the Communists in China killed thirty-five million. The Nazis killed over

Victims of the Nazis at Auschwitz

twenty million and no doubt would have killed millions more had they not been defeated.[1]

So it is important to learn the lesson and to get it right.

After coming to power by democratic and constitu-

---

[1] See Courtois 1999, pp. x, 4: contributors to that volume variously estimate the Communist death toll to be from 85 million to 100 million. See also Rummel 1997, Section II. Rummel at http://www.hawaii.edu/powerkills/ has updated numbers. For example, new data on deliberately caused famines in the People's Republic of China under Mao led Rummel to revise the death toll for communist China upwards to 76,702,000.

tional means in 1933, the Nazis quickly turned Germany into a dictatorship. For six years they devoted their energies to preparing for war, which began in 1939. During the war in which every human and economic resource was needed for military purposes, the Nazis devoted huge amounts of resources in an attempt to exterminate Jews, gypsies, Slavs, and others.

Domestic dictatorship, international war, the Holocaust. All are terrible. But what exactly *is* the lesson of history here? How could a civilized European nation plunge itself and the world into such a horror?

4. Five weak explanations for National Socialism

a) A common explanation is that the Germans lost World War I. They were bitter over the loss and the harsh punitive measures the victors imposed in the Versailles Treaty. There is a grain of truth here, but this is a very weak explanation. One reason why it is weak is that many countries lose bitter wars, but they do not respond by electing Adolf Hitlers to power. Another reason is that Germany's losing the war does not explain Italy. In the 1920s Italy turned to Benito Mussolini and his fascist version of National Socialism. But Italy was on the winning side of World War I. So if one of the winners of World War I became fascist, and one of the losers also became fascist, then whether one lost or won the war is not the significant factor here.

b) Another explanation holds that Germany's economic troubles of the 1920s were the cause of National Socialism. Here again there is a grain of truth, but again this is a weak explanation. Many countries suffer economic malaise, but they do not turn to National Socialism for the solution. There is also the phenomenon of Nazi and neo-Nazi movements throughout the twentieth century in relatively prosperous countries. Very few countries suffering economic difficulties go

Nazi, and there are plenty of Nazi-sympathizers in prosperous nations.

c) Another weak explanation suggests that there is something innately wrong with Germans, that history shows that they are inherently militaristic, bloodthirsty, and genocidal—and the Nazis merely tapped into and exaggerated innate German tendencies. This kind of explanation is an insult of course to the many Germans who were appalled by National Socialism, who opposed it and fought it vigorously. And it does not explain how National Socialism has appealed to people of many races and ethnicities. In 2005, *Mein Kampf* was a bestseller in the country of Turkey.[2] Do we want to suggest that the Turks are inherently bloodthirsty and genocidal? I do not think so.

d) Another weak explanation holds that Nazism is explained by the personal neuroses and psychoses of the Nazi leadership. The argument here is that Hitler was bitterly disappointed by being rejected for art school—or that he was a repressed homosexual—or that his right-hand man, Josef Goebbels was compensating for his below-average height and having a club foot. Again, this is a poor explanation. How many art-school rejects become Nazis? How many repressed homosexuals or handicapped men become Nazis? This explanation also ignores the large number of powerful Nazis who were neither homosexual nor short nor particularly interested in art.

e) Any of the above explanations can works together with a suggestion that the Nazis were a product of modern communications technologies—that as masters of rhetoric and propaganda the Nazis succeeded in fooling millions of Germans about their agenda and manipulated their way into power.

I have some sympathy for this way of thinking, for it is the kind of explanation that comes naturally to those of us raised in liberal democracies. When I first started learning

---

[2] "Mein Kampf a Bestseller in Turkey," April 20, 2005. http://www.windsofchange.net/archives/006690.php. Viewed August 24, 2009.

about the Nazis, I thought they must have been insane. It is hard to imagine that such horror could be anything but the products of deranged minds manipulating the masses. But here I want to suggest two reasons why I think it is not a good idea to dismiss the Nazis merely as manipulators.

The first is that the Nazis achieved power though democratic and constitutional methods. When the party was formed in 1920, it was a small, fringe party. But it spoke to the beliefs and aspirations of millions of Germans. And in the 1920s, the Germans were, arguably, the most educated nation in the world with the highest levels of literacy, numbers of years of schooling, newspaper readership, political awareness, and so on. It was in an *educated* nation that the Nazis achieved increasing success in elections through the 1920s, spreading their message far and wide, until they made their major break-throughs in the early 1930s. Millions of voters in a democracy may be wrong, but it is unlikely that they were all deluded. A better explanation is that they knew what they were voting for and thought it the best course of action. And that is what I will be arguing.

But millions of people do not decide spontaneously to vote for this party or that. A mass political movement requires that much cultural groundwork be done over the course of many years. And this is where intellectuals do their work. A culture's intellectuals develop and articulate a culture's ideals, its goals, its aspirations. In books, speeches, sermons, and radio broadcasts, intellectuals are a culture's opinion-shapers. It is intellectuals who write the opinion pieces in the mass newspapers, who are the professors at the universities, the universities where teachers and preachers are trained, where politicians and lawyers and scientists and physicians get their education.

This leads us to the other reason why it is a weak explanation to say the Nazis were simply deranged and lucked or manipulated their way into political power. Consider the following list of intellectuals who supported the Nazis long before they came to power. These intellectuals represent a "Who's Who" list of powerful minds and cultural leaders:

Philipp Lenard won the Nobel Prize for Physics in 1905.

Gerhart Hauptmann won the Nobel Prize for Literature in 1912. Hauptmann once met Hitler and described their brief handshake as "the greatest moment of my life."

Johannes Stark won the Nobel Prize for Physics in 1919.

That is three Nobel Prize winners.

Then there is Dr. Oswald Spengler, author of the historical bestseller *The Decline of the West* (1918). Spengler's books sold in the millions, and he was perhaps the most famous intellectual in Germany in the 1920s.

Then there is Moeller van den Bruck, another famous public intellectual of the 1920s. His book *The Third Reich* (1923) provided a theoretical rationale for National Socialism and was, like Spengler's books, a consistent best-seller throughout the 1920s.

Then there is Dr. Carl Schmitt (1888-1985), probably the sharpest legal and political mind of his generation. Schmitt's books are still widely read and discussed by political theoreticians of all stripes and are recognized as twentieth century classics.

And to round out this initial list, there is philosopher Martin Heidegger. Already in the 1920s Heidegger was being hailed as the brightest philosopher of his generation, which is especially significant in a philosophical nation such as Germany. That assessment has held over

Martin Heidegger

the course of the twentieth century. Ask professional philosophers of today to name the five most significant philosophers of the twentieth century and, whether they love him or loathe him, most will include Heidegger on the list.

These seven men are among the most intelligent and powerful minds in Germany in the decade before the Nazis came to power. They are leading figures in German intellectual culture, spanning the arts, science, history, law, politics, and philosophy.[3] All of them, to one degree or another, supported National Socialism. Was Hitler smart enough to fool all of these highly intelligent men? Or is it more likely that they knew what they believed and supported National Socialism because they thought it was true?[4]

5. Explaining Nazism philosophically

I want to suggest a better explanation: The primary cause of

---

[3] Weinreich 1999 (pp. 13-16) gives a wide-ranging list of professors and intellectuals who supported Hitler prior to 1933. See also Rohkrämer 2005 for a clear discussion of the role of Heidegger and the many other philosophers who gave enthusiastic support to the Nazis. Earl Shorris (2007) describes Germany of the time as "a society richer in the knowledge of the humanities than perhaps any other in modern times. Among those people who rose to the top of the Nazi government were students of humanities, former scholars. Joseph Goebbels had studied history and literature at the University of Heidelberg. Reinhard (Hangman) Heydrich was the child of a pianist and an opera singer who founded a conservatory. Ernst Kaltenbrunner studied law at the University of Prague. More than a third of the members of the Vienna Philharmonic belonged to the Nazi Party. Albert Speer, who ran the business side of the Nazi war machine, was an architect." Gottlob Frege (1848-1925), the great logician and philosopher of mathematics, can be added to this list. Frege was an anti-Semite and later in life named Adolf Hitler as one of his heroes; see Reuben Hersh, *What Is Mathematics, Really?* (Oxford University Press, 1997), p. 241.

[4] Albert Speer described "the event that led me to [Hitler]," which was a speech Hitler gave to the College of Engineering in Berlin. Speer expected the talk to be "a bombastic harangue" but it turned out to be a "reasoned lecture" (quoted in Orlow 1969, p. 199).

Nazism lies in *philosophy*. Not economics, not psychology, and not even politics.

National Socialism was first a philosophy of life believed and advocated by highly intelligent men and women. Professors, public intellectuals, Nobel Prize-winners—all powerful minds working at the cutting edges of their disciplines. It was they who shaped the intellectual culture of Germany in the 1920s and who convinced millions of Germans that National Socialism was the best hope for Germany's future.

That is not to say that there were no other contributing factors. The legacy of World War I, persistent economic troubles, modern communication technologies, and the personal psychologies of the Nazi leadership did play a role. But the *most* significant factor was the power of a set of abstract, philosophical ideas. National Socialism was a philosophy-intensive movement.

I will up the ante further.

I also want to suggest that the Nazi intellectuals and their followers thought of themselves as *idealists* and as *crusaders for a noble cause*. This may be even harder to accept. The National Socialists in the 1920s were passionate men and women who thought that the world was in a crisis and that a moral revolution was called for. They believed their ideas to be true, beautiful, noble, and the only hope for the world.[5] Yes, Nazi ideology contained major elements of harshness, even brutality—but what if an important truth about the world is that it is harsh and brutal?

[5] As did many foreign observers, e.g., the Anglican clergymen who expressed "boundless admiration for the moral and ethical side of the National Social programme, its clear-cut stand for religion and Christianity, and its ethical principles, such as its fight against cruelty to animals, vivisections, sexual offenses, etc." (quoted in Manchester 1989, p. 82).

It may be hard to believe that the Nazis thought of themselves as noble idealists, especially with our after-the-fact knowledge of the horrible destructiveness of Nazism. It may be especially hard for those of us raised in Western liberal democracies to believe it—since from the cradle we've been raised to believe that freedom, equality, and peace are almost self-evidently good.

But what if they are not self-evidently good? Let me play the Devil's advocate.

How long have human beings existed? Most anthropologists say *Homo sapiens* has existed for well over 100,000 years, perhaps as long as 200,000 years. For how much of that time have freedom, equality, and peace been the norm? Democratic experiments were tried in ancient Greece for a few centuries. A little later, republican experiments were tried in ancient Rome—again for a few centuries. But Greece and Rome both failed: the Greeks were conquered by the Romans, and the Romans descended into authoritarian decadence before themselves being conquered. And there have been a few smaller and relatively brief republican city states—Renaissance Venice, Florence, and in the Baltic. That is a few short-lived experiments in over 100,000 years—not very impressive.

So now we imagine ourselves in Europe in the earliest decades of the twentieth century: democratic republicanism has been resurrected and is being tried again, for example in the United States of America. How successful have the modern experiments been? Come the 1920s, the United States is only about 150 years old. That means that it has survived for less time than the Greek democracies or the Roman Republic. The U.S. lasted only 90 years before it plunged into a brutal Civil War, the reverberations of which are still being felt early in the twentieth century. In the 1920s the U.S. is itself experiencing economic uncertainty and is shortly to plunge into its Great Depression. Even in the United States, many intellectuals are suggesting that capitalism and liberalism are finished and that some form of centralized authority led by a strong man is the future. So in the 1920s, just how strong is the case for liberty, democracy, republicanism, and capitalism?[6]

What if a culture's brightest thinkers believe that democracy is a historical blip? What if they come to believe that the lesson of history is that what people need is structure and strong leadership? What if they believe that history shows that some cultures are obviously superior—superior in their arts, their science and technology, and their religion? What if they believe that history teaches that we live in a harsh world of conflict and that in such a world strength and assertiveness against one's enemies are essential to survive? Or even more strongly than that—that peace makes people soft and that it is conflict and war that brings out the best in people, making them tough, vigorous, and willing to fight for their ideals and if necessary *die* for them?[7]

I am suggesting that a set of ideals was primarily responsible for the rise of Nazism.[8] I think those ideals are extraordinarily false and terribly destructive—but that is not how millions of intelligent, educated, even in many cases well-meaning Germans saw them.

But why do I call them a set of ideals? Why not just say the Nazis had some ideas—of course they had some ideas with which to bewitch the masses—but basically they just wanted power and were effective at using those ideas to get power?

Well, of course the Nazis wanted power. What politician doesn't want power? But if you are only out for power,

---

[6] "Few of the supporters of Weimar understood that for many Germans the fundamental political issue in 1930 was the pluralistic system of politics itself, not substantive issues within the system" (Orlow 1969, p. 186).

[7] E.g., Immanuel Kant: "a prolonged peace favours the predominance of a mere commercial spirit, and with it a debasing self-interest, cowardice, and effeminacy, and tends to degrade the character of the nation" (1951 [1790], p. 28). See Appendix 4 for quotations on German militarism.

[8] Contra, e.g., Helmut Kuhn (1963, p. 310), who asserts that the Nazis *perverted* German philosophy.

think about how you go about getting it in a democracy. The best way is to identify the established political parties, join one of the powerful ones, and work your way up the ranks to the top.

Here is an analogy: In the United States, the two major parties are the Democratic and Republican parties. So if you are young and ambitious and you want a realistic chance at becoming a Senator or even President in your lifetime, you join one of those two parties. What you do *not* do is join a fringe party. What you do *not* do is start your own party—say, the Midwestern Farmer's Union Party, out in the middle of nowhere. The only reason you would start the Midwestern Farmer's Union Party is that you are a true believer in the ideals of Midwestern Farming and think you cannot achieve your ideals by joining the established parties.

But that describes the Nazis exactly. They did *not* join the Social Democrats or any of the established political parties. They set up their own fringe party, initially based in the south of Germany and away from the center of power in Berlin. They were true believers in a cause. They did not want power if it meant compromising their ideals by joining with an established party. They wanted power—but power to achieve what they took to be high ideals.

So what was this obscure political party formed in Munich in 1920, and what did it stand for?

Part 3. National Socialist Philosophy

6. The Nazi Party Program

The Nazi Party grew out of the D.A.P., the German Workers' Party. Its goal according to one of its founders, Gottfried Feder, "was to reconcile nationalism and socialism." It was a lecture by Feder in 1919 that attracted Adolf Hitler to the party. Within a year the party changed its name in order to have a name that expressed more accurately its core principles: The new name was the National Socialist German Work-

Adolf Hitler

ers' Party. At a rally in Munich in 1920 involving over 2,000 participants, the party announced its platform—a twenty-five point program.[9] The main authors of the program were Feder, Adolf Hitler, and a third man, Anton Drexler. To understand what National Socialism stood for, the main points of the Program are worth looking at more closely.

7. Collectivism, not individualism

A major theme of the Program is a stress upon collectivism and a rejection of individualism.

---

[9] See Appendix 1 for the twenty-five point *Program of the National Socialist German Workers' Party*.

Point number 10 of the Program, for example, says "It must be the first duty of every citizen to perform mental or physical work. Individual activity must not violate the general interest, but must be exercised within the framework of the community, and for the general good."

National Socialism thus consciously rejects Western liberal individualism with its emphasis on the rights to life, liberty, and the pursuit of happiness—all of which are individualistic rights. Nazism is collectivistic: it does not hold that individuals have their own lives to live and happiness to pursue. Rather, individuals should work for the community out of a sense of duty; they serve the general good, to which they subordinate their personal lives.

Point 24 of the Program returns to this theme and emphasizes it strongly: "THE COMMON INTEREST BEFORE SELF-INTEREST." The bold print and capitalization are in the original, for emphasis.

8. Economic socialism, not capitalism

The second theme of the Program is a stress upon socialism and a strong rejection of capitalism.

Numerically, socialism is the most emphasized theme in the Nazi Program, for over half of the Program's twenty-five points—fourteen out of the twenty-five, to be exact—itemize economically socialist demands.

Point 11 calls for the abolition of all income gained by loaning money at interest.

Point 12 demands the confiscation of all profits earned by German businesses during World War I.

Point 13 demands the nationalization of all corporations.

Point 14 demands profit-sharing in large industrial enterprises.

Point 15 demands the generous development of state-run old-age insurance.

Point 16 calls for the immediate socialization of the huge department stores.

And so on.

So strong was the Nazi party's commitment to socialism that in 1921 the party entered into negotiations to merge with another socialist party, the German Socialist Party. The negotiations fell though, but the economic socialism remained a consistent Nazi theme through the 1920s and 30s.

For example, here is Adolf Hitler in a speech in 1927:

> We are socialists, we are enemies of today's capitalistic economic system for the exploitation of the economically weak, with its unfair salaries, with its unseemly evaluation of a human being according to wealth and property instead of responsibility and performance, and we are all determined to destroy this system under all conditions.[10]

Even more strongly, Josef Goebbels hated capitalism and urged socialism. Dr. Josef Goebbels was perhaps the most brilliant and educated of all the Nazi politicians. Once the Nazis came to power he was to be one of the most powerful of the very top Nazis—perhaps number two or three after Hitler himself. But Goebbels' commitment to National Socialist principles began much earlier. He received a wide-ranging classical education by attending five universities in Germany, eventually receiving a Ph.D. in literature and philosophy from

Dr. Joseph Goebbels

---

[10] May 1, 1927; quoted in Toland 1976, p. 306.

Heidelberg University in 1921. During his graduate student days he absorbed and agreed with much of the writings of communists Karl Marx and Friedrich Engels. Damning those he called "the money pigs of capitalist democracy,"[11] Goebbels in speeches and pamphlets regularly declaimed that "Money has made slaves of us."[12] "Money," he argued, "is the curse of mankind. It smothers the seed of everything great and good. Every penny is sticky with sweat and blood." And in language that could be right out of the writings of Karl Marx, Goebbels believed fervently: "The worker in a capitalist state—and that is his deepest misfortune—is no longer a living human being, a creator, a maker. He has become a machine. A number, a cog in the machine without sense or understanding. He is alienated from what he produces."[13]

The Nazi solution, then, is strong socialism.[14] The state should control the economy, organizing its production and distribution in the collective interest.[15]

9. Nationalism, not internationalism or cosmopolitanism

This raises a question. So far the Nazi Program emphasizes that collectivism and socialism take priority over the individual—but which collective or social grouping has priority? Here the Nazi Program emphatically defines its collectivism and socialism in nationalistic terms. Individuals belong primarily to their ethnic and racial groups, those ethnic and racial groups giving them their core identities.

---

[11] Quoted in Orlow 1969, p. 87.

[12] Goebbels 1929, in Mosse ed., 1966, p. 107.

[13] Goebbels 1932, "Those Damned Nazis" pamphlet.

[14] See Appendix 2 for more quotations from Nazi leaders on the socialism of National Socialism.

[15] This explains why the Nazi SA "staged joint rallies with the Communists and planned campaigns to win over the KDP members well into 1929 and 1930" (Orlow 1969, p. 210).

In the 1920 Program, seven of the twenty-five points speak directly to this issue. This issue is moderately complicated, because the Nazis have three enemies in mind against whom they want to distinguish themselves.

First they reject Marxist socialism or any socialism that puts economic groupings first. As much as the Nazis hate capitalism, they do not see the world as a battle between economic groups. The Marxists, as they see it, are obsessed with and too narrowly focused on money. To the Nazis money is only part of the battle—the *major* battle is between different racial and cultural groups with different biological histories, languages, values, laws, and religions. The battle is between Germans—with their particular biological inheritance and cultural history—against all other racial cultures.

Second, the Nazis reject cosmopolitanism, an ideal of Western liberals who believe that all humans are essentially the same wherever one travels in the world, and who believe that one should strive to be a citizen of the world, someone who can be at home anywhere.

The Nazis are *nationalists*, by contrast, and they reject any form of internationalism or cosmopolitanism.[16]

These themes explain the design of the Nazis' swastika flag, as a symbolic integration of the socialism and the nationalism. Red is symbolic of socialism, white is symbolic of nationalism, and the swastika is, according to Hitler, representative of the Aryan struggle for racial and cultural supremacy against those who are trying to destroy the Germans.

Consequently, in the Nazi Program of 1920 we find many points about German national identity and asserting German needs and goals.

---

[16] As Goebbels put it in his 1929 *Michael*, which sold well and went through seventeen editions: "Race is the matrix of all creative forces. Humanity—that is a mere supposition. Reality is only the Volk. Humanity is nothing but a multitude of peoples. A people is an organic entity" (Goebbels 1929, in Mosse ed., 1966, p. 106).

Point 1 demands the unification of all ethnic Germans into a greater Germany.

Point 8 demands that immigration by non-Germans be halted and that all those who have immigrated recently be expelled from the country.

Public offices can be open only to citizens, and Point 3 defines citizenship in terms of the possession of German blood.

And the possession of German blood is defined carefully to reject a third target of the Nazis, those whom they hate even more than the Marxists or the liberal capitalists—and that is the Jews.[17]

Point 3 of the Program denies that Jews can be racial comrades of Germans, and this in combination with the other points in the Program effectively shuts the Jews out of German life.

A widely-used Nazi propaganda poster displayed a dragon with three heads wearing hats representing the communist, the international capitalist, and the Jew—the enemies the pure German warrior must defeat.

From the beginning of the Party in 1920 then, the pro-German nationalism and the strong anti-Semitic themes are, like the collectivism and the socialism, core Nazi themes.

While the 1920 Program only mentions the Jews twice and seems to advocate only that the Jews be forced to leave Germany, within a few years the Nazi leadership had clearly begun to consider harsher measures. In 1925, for example, Hitler published *Mein Kampf*, a book that sold increasingly

---

[17] Michael Mack's *German Idealism and the Jew* (University of Chicago Press, 2003) is a study of the role German philosophers, historians, and other intellectuals, including Kant, Hegel, Marx, and others, played in developing and promoting anti-Semitism. See Appendix 3 for further quotations.

well as the Nazis rose to power. Hitler variously describes the Jews as an "octopus," as "a parasite on the body of other nations," as a "vampire," as a "spider" that was "suck[ing] the blood out of the people's pores," and as having taken over the German state. To free the German *Volk*, consequently, Hitler calls for the "elimination of the existing Jewish one" and "the end of this parasite upon the nations."[18]

10. Authoritarianism, not liberal democracy

So far we have three major themes in the Nazi Program: collectivism, socialism, and nationalism. The next question is: How do the Nazis believe this is to be achieved?

As early as 1920 the Nazis are clear that they are no friends of democracy, liberalism, or republicanism. They favor strong authoritarianism and centralized power.

Point 23 calls for censorship and government control of all newspapers.

Point 24 suggests limitations on religions that do not fit the Nazis' goals.

Point 25 calls for centralization and unconditional power: "we demand the creation of a strong central power in Germany. A central political parliament should possess unconditional authority over the entire Reich, and its organization in general."

These points in combination with the economically socialist points earlier are to give the government total control over all aspects of society.

Throughout the 1920s the Nazis are unapologetic about wanting to eliminate liberalism, democracy, and republicanism. Goebbels for example put it bluntly and publicly: "Never do the people rule themselves. This madness has been

---

[18] Hitler 1925, pp. 623, 305, 327, 193, 453, and 327.

invented by liberalism. Behind its concept of the sovereignty of the people hide the most corrupt rogues, who do not want to be recognized."[19]

In *Mein Kampf*, Hitler agreed entirely: "There must be no majority decisions." Instead, *"the decisions will be made by one man."*[20] So, Goebbels continued, "We shall create a power-group with which we can conquer this state. And then ruthlessly and brutally, using the State's prerogatives, we shall enforce our will and our programme." Again from Goebbels:

> History has seen repeatedly how a young, de-
> termined minority has overthrown the rule of a
> corrupt and rotten majority, and then used for
> a time the State and its means of power in order
> to bring about by dictatorship ... and force the
> conditions necessary to complete the conquest
> and to impose new ideas.[21]

The Nazis were very clear from the outset what they were in favor of, what they opposed, and how they planned to exercise power once they achieved it: socialism, national-ism, racial identity and purification—and a strong, centralized power to make it happen.

11. Idealism, not politics as usual

It is important to emphasize that the Nazis put their program forward forthrightly and as a noble—even spiritual—ideal to achieve. They promised not merely another political platform, but a whole philosophy of life that, as they and their followers believed, promised renewal. And they called upon Germans to exercise the highest virtues of altruism and self-sacrifice for the good of society to bring about that renewal.

Program point 10 urges individuals to put the common good of Germany before their self interest. Point 24 repeats it.

---

[19] Goebbels 1929, in Mosse ed., 1966, p. 105.
[20] Hitler 1925, p. 449.
[21] Goebbels 1927, quoted in Irving 1999, p. 117.

Hitler and Goebbels repeatedly urge Nazism as a spiritual and ideal vision in contrast to the usual power-grubbing politics of the day.

In *Mein Kampf*, Hitler insisted that "All force which does not spring from a firm spiritual foundation will be hesitating and uncertain. It lacks the stability which can only rest on a fanatical view of life."[22]

He called upon individuals not to be egoistic but be willing to sacrifice: "the preservation of the existence of a species presupposes a spirit of sacrifice in the individual."[23]

In Goebbels's autobiographical novel, *Michael*, a book that sold out of seventeen editions, the leading character is explicitly likened to Jesus Christ: Michael is the 'Christ-socialist' who sacrifices himself out of love for mankind—and Goebbels urges that noble Germans be willing to do the same.[24] A widely-used Nazi poster featured a religiously spiritual figure with its arm encircling a young Nazi soldier.

Hitler regularly praised Germans for their spirit of altruism: "this state of mind, which subordinates the interests of the ego to the conservation of the community, is really the first premise for every truly human culture."[25] Altruism, he believed, is a trait more pronounced in Germans than in any

---

[22] Hitler 1925, p. 222.
[23] Hitler 1925, p. 151.
[24] Goebbels 1929, in Mosse ed., 1966, p. 108.
[25] Hitler 1925, 298. Hitler distinguishes altruism from "egoism and selfishness" and also labels it "Idealism. By this we understand only the individual's capacity to make sacrifices for the community" (1925, p. 28). Egoism and the pursuit of happiness he sees as the great threat: "As soon as egoism becomes the ruler of a people, the bonds of order are loosened and in the chase after their own happiness men fall from heaven into a real hell" (1925, p. 300).

other culture, which is why he claimed to be so optimistic about Germany's future.

This message of National Socialism as a moral ideal and a spiritual crusade was appealing to many, many Germans—and especially the young. By 1925 the party membership in the north was mostly young: two-thirds of the members were under thirty years of age, and in a few years the Nazis had attracted a large following among university students.

Goebbels especially called out to the idealistic young to be the heart of the Nazi future in Germany:

> The old ones don't even want to understand that we young people even exist. They defend their power to the last. But one day they will be defeated after all. Youth finally must be victorious. We young ones, we shall attack. The attacker is always stronger than the defender. If we free ourselves, we can also liberate the whole working class. And the liberated working class will release the Fatherland from its chains.[26]

12. Nazi democratic success

For the Nazis, the clear, firm, and passionate advocacy of their political goals, along with efficient organization and propaganda, brought them increasing democratic success in Germany.

After years of work, by 1928 the party had only twelve seats in the Reichstag, Germany's national parliament. But in the election of September 1930, they increased that number to 107 seats. Less than two years later, in the election of July 1932, they increased that number dramatically to 230 seats. A few months later they lost thirty-four seats in a November election and now had 196. But in January of 1933, Hitler was

---

[26] Goebbels 1929, p. 111.

appointed Chancellor of Germany, one of the two highest positions in the land, and the Nazis were in a position to consolidate their power. In March of 1933 they called yet another election in order to get a clear mandate from the German people about their plans for Germany. The election had a huge turnout and the Nazis scored huge gains, winning 43.9% of the popular vote and 288 seats in the Reichstag. 288 seats are more seats than their next three competitors combined.

Table 1. Germany: March 5, 1933 election. Seats in the Reichstag:[27]

NSDAP (National Socialist)	288
SPD (Socialist)	120
KPD (Communist)	81
Zentrum (Center, Catholic)	73
Kampfront SWR (Nationalist)	52
Bayerische Volkspartei	19
Deutsche Staatspartei	5
Christlich-Sozialer Volksdienst	4
Deutsche Volkspartei (Nationalist)	2
Deutsche Bauernpartei	2
Württembergerische Landbund	1

By early 1933, the National Socialist German Workers' Party was in control.

Early NSDAP leaders

[27] Craig 1978, p. 576.

Part 4. The Nazis in Power

13. Political controls

As the Nazis had promised, they moved quickly to transform Germany from a constitutional democracy into an authoritarian dictatorship. An early step they took was to eliminate rival political parties. Some were banned outright; the rest were pressured to dissolve themselves; and in July of 1933, the Nazi government banned the formation of new political parties.

Hitler, *der Führer*

In 1934, the Nazis further consolidated their power and augmented Hitler's. Hitler had almost always had a strong grip on the internal politics of the Nazi party, but it had not been absolute. 1934 brought an internal purge and an elimination of Hitler's rivals. The triggering event was Ernst Röhm's attempted rebellion. Röhm had been head of the SA, the *Sturmabteilung* or Storm Division, the paramilitary wing of the party. Röhm had used his position to form a rival power bloc within the party and planned a rebellion. Hitler was warned of the rebellion ahead of time and was able to suppress it. In the purge that followed, forty-three conspirators and rivals were executed. Along with the purge, there were many unofficial assassinations as old scores were settled. The result of the blood-letting was a Nazi party even more strongly united around Adolf Hitler.

In August of the same year, President Hindenburg died. Paul von Hindenburg had been the grand old man of German politics, holding the office of the presidency, which was along with the chancellorship one of the two highest political offices in the land. Upon Hindenburg's death, Hitler merged the positions of president and chancellor, thus augmenting his power further. In a nation-wide plebiscite to confirm the merging of the two positions, almost 90% of Germans voted in favor of granting Hitler greater powers.

The Nazis now controlled all the major political offices, they had cleaned house internally, and they had eliminated all rival parties. In firm control, they next set about re-shaping all of German society.

14. Education

Political tools such as physical force and authoritarian laws are necessary tools for a dictatorship, but long-term control of a people also requires control of their minds. The Nazis recognized this and made re-shaping Germany's educational system a priority. They already had a good head-start.

When the National Socialists came to power in 1933, about 2.5 million Germans were members of the Nazi Party. Seven percent of the Party's members were from the upper class, seven percent were peasants, thirty-five percent were industrial workers, and fifty-one percent were from the professional and middle class. Surprisingly, in the latter group, the professional and middle class, the largest occupational group represented was elementary school teachers. Hitler and the Nazis thus already had a core group of committed followers in a position to help them shape the minds of the next generation.

The general purpose of education

The Nazis had a particular kind of youth in mind. As early as 1925, Hitler had written in *Mein Kampf*: "the folkish state must not adjust its entire educational work primarily to the inoculation of mere knowledge, but to the breeding of absolutely healthy bodies. The training of mental abilities is only secondary."[28]

Come 1933 and power, Hitler repeatedly made it even clearer what kind of healthy bodies he wanted the educational system to produce:

> My program for educating youth is hard. Weakness must be hammered away. In my castles of the Teutonic Order a youth will grow up before which the world will tremble. I want a brutal, domineering, fearless, cruel youth. Youth must be all that. It must bear pain. There must be nothing weak and gentle about it. The free, splendid beast of prey must once again flash from its eyes ... That is how I will eradicate thousands of years of human domestication ... That is how I will create the New Order.

Intellectual training was less emphasized than physical training, but it was not omitted. Students were trained in Nazi ideology, studied German history from a National Socialist perspective, learned political activism, and trained themselves to develop a selfless, obedient, duty-oriented moral character. The curriculum was revised, textbooks re-written, and teachers trained as servants of the cause. Early in the Nazi reign, teachers were declared to be civil servants and required to join the National Socialist Teachers League, swearing an oath of absolute fidelity to Adolf Hitler.

---

[28] Hitler 1925, p. 408.

The Hitler Youth

In addition to transforming the formal school system, the Nazis put great emphasis on the Hitler Youth organization. The Nazi Party's youth organization had been formed in 1922, early in the party's history, and acquired its Hitler Youth name in 1926. The purpose of the Hitler Youth was to train a cadre of devoted young followers outside the formal school system. Once the Nazis came to power, the formal German school system and the Hitler Youth became comple-

A Youth and the Führer

mentary training and indoctrination programs.

Boys could enter the program when they were age six, though official training began at age ten. All members of the Hitler Youth swore this oath: "In the presence of this blood-banner, which represents our Führer, I swear to devote all my energies and my strength to the savior of our country, Adolf Hitler. I am ready and willing to give up my life for him, so help me God."[29]

Full membership and systematic training began at age fourteen and included the ability to take a physical beating without whining. Brutal fighting sessions among the boys were common and encouraged. As Hitler had put it in *Mein Kampf*, "But above all, the young, healthy body must also learn to suffer blows."[30] If a boy was unable to withstand the pain or pressure, he was embarrassed in front of his peers. Those who succeeded, though, received accolades, a sense of belonging to a great cause, and useful symbols of their status, such as a special dagger.

[29] Quoted in Shirer 1962, p. 253.
[30] Hitler 1925, p. 410.

Parallel programs existed for girls. The League of Young Girls was established for girls ten to fourteen years of age. The fourteen-to-eighteen-year-old girls' group of the Hitler Youth was the Bund Deutscher Mädel, or League of German Girls. From seventeen to twenty-one years of age, young Aryan women were members of Faith and Beauty. Instruction focused on home, family, and the duty to bear children. The girls' training was similar to the boys', including wearing military-style uniforms, engaging in soldier-like activities, and learning Nazi ideology and activism.

Although the youth were encouraged to question their parents and their non-Nazi teachers, *within* the Hitler Youth absolute obedience was demanded. Despite this, membership in the Hitler Youth was *appealing* to many young Germans. Summer camps and parades were regular activities for the Hitler Youth. There was also the feeling of camaraderie and the sense of developing a sense of self-discipline, loyalty, and honor. Membership came to be considered to be a badge of honor—and, as the Nazi Party came closer to achieving power, membership even became a status symbol.

In 1932, the year before the Nazis came to power, the Hitler Youth had 107,956 members—or five percent of the German youth population. Within a year, membership had swollen to well over two million members.

In 1936, membership in the Hitler Youth became mandatory. All other youth groups had ceased to exist, been absorbed into the Hitler Youth, or abolished. And by 1939, the year that World War II was to begin, membership in the Hitler Youth reached almost eight million members.

The universities

The Nazis had also achieved great success with older students, those of university age.

Well before Hitler came to power, Nazi student groups

existed at universities all over Germany. Before 1933, it was common for students to come to classes wearing brown shirts and swastika armbands, and in many cases it was the most intelligent and idealistic university students who were the most activist and outspoken supporters of National Socialism.

The students also had many allies among their professors.

When the National Socialists took power, they prohibited all Jews from holding academic positions—this resulted in the firing of hundreds of tenured Jewish professors, including several Nobel Laureates. To their credit, many other professors resigned in protest or emigrated. But such professors were in the small minority.[31]

A large majority of university professors remained on the job, either silently accepting the new regime or even actively supporting it. In 1933, for example, 960 professors, including prominent figures such as philosopher Martin Heidegger, made a public proclamation of their support for Adolf Hitler and the National Socialist regime.[32]

---

[31] "But in numbers the *émigrés* were not to be compared with the leading figures in every field of intellectual endeavour who hailed the advent of National Socialism and pledged support to its Führer with every evidence of enthusiasm" (Craig 1978, p. 639).

[32] Shirer 1962, p. 251. Rohkrämer notes the following: "Association with National Socialism was also widespread among philosophers. While twenty philosophy professors were forced out of their positions, about thirty joined the Nazi Party in 1933 and almost half became party members by 1940" (Rohkrämer 2005, p. 171). On Heidegger in particular, given his high profile in the landscape of 20th-century philosophy, "'Martin Heidegger? A Nazi, of course a Nazi!' On a purely factual level, this exclamation by Jürgen Habermas is fully correct. Contrary to what Heidegger and Heideggerians have long maintained, historical research has demonstrated beyond doubt Heidegger's early enthusiasm for National Socialism. Heidegger sympathized with the Nazis before 1933, he actively maneuvered to become rector, he publicly joined the Nazi Party on May Day, and the ceremony around his Rectoral Address included Nazi flags and the singing of the 'Horst Wessel Song.' While Jews and political opponents were removed from the university (like his teacher Edmund Husserl) or even forced to flee the country (like his intimate friend Hannah Arendt), Heidegger showed his enthusiastic support for the destruction of the Weimar Republic and for the new regime. He praised the Führer principle for the university sector, while striving to attain

15. Censorship

What the Nazis established for the schools and universities they attempted to establish for German society at large, by means of sweeping government regulations on media and outright censorship. The world of schools and education was only an important microcosm of the Nazis' plans for all of German society.

Joseph Goebbels, Germany's new propaganda chief, put it this way: Any book or work of art "which acts subversively on our future or strikes at the root of German thought, the German home and the driving forces of our people" should be destroyed.

The great symbolic statement of what was to come occurred early in the Nazi regime—the May 10, 1933 book burnings, just a few months after the Nazis assumed power. In the Unter den Linden, an open square across from the University of Berlin, roughly 20,000 books were burned in a huge bonfire. Goebbels spoke at the event to 40,000 cheering spectators. Some of the authors whose books were destroyed were Thomas Mann, Albert Einstein, Jack London, Helen Keller, H. G. Wells, Sigmund Freud, Émile Zola, and Marcel Proust.

An important and sometimes overlooked fact about the book burnings is that they were not instigated by the Nazi

---

such a position for himself. In speeches and newspaper articles he identified himself with Hitler's rule, going so far as to state in autumn 1933 that 'the Führer himself and alone is and will be Germany's only reality and its law.' He not only approved in principle of the Nazi cleansing, but also tried to use the new regime to destroy the academic careers of colleagues, for example by initiating a Gestapo investigation" (Rohkrämer 2005, pp. 172-173).

government. Nor were they instigated by non-intellectual thugs. The book burnings were instigated by university students. The Nazi Party's *student* organization conceived and carried out book burnings all across the country—book bonfires burned brightly that night in every German university city. The professors had taught their students well.

Goebbels's official title was Minister of the Reich Chamber of Culture. The Reich Chamber of Culture controlled seven cultural spheres: fine arts, music, theater, literature, the press, radio, and films. This gave him power over all the major media in Germany and enabled him to use his formidable talent for propaganda effectively. He quickly established regulations that anyone working in any of those fields had to become a member of the Nazi party and join the respective chamber. The purpose of the regulations was, as Goebbels put it:

> In order to pursue a policy of German culture, it is necessary to gather together the creative artists in all spheres into a unified organization under the leadership of the Reich. The Reich must not only determine the lines of progress, mental and spiritual, but also lead and organize the professions.[33]

In the realm of art, Hitler and Goebbels attempted to cleanse Germany of modern art and to replace it with "Germanic" art. Classical plays, music, and operas, as well as Hollywood B-movies were still allowed, but galleries exhibiting modern art were shut down.

Newspapers received close supervision. The Reich Press Law of 1933 prohibited editors of newspapers from marrying Jews, and required that editors meet daily with the Propaganda Ministry to ensure that no misleading stories were published. Essentially, this meant that the government told the

---

[33] Quoted in Shirer 1962, p. 241.

newspapers what they could and could not print.

Likewise, radio was taken over in 1933 by another branch of the Propaganda Ministry, the Chamber of Radio.

The Chamber of Films took over the content of the film industry, though it left the production of films up to private firms.

In all areas of arts and culture, uncooperative editors, writers, and performers were ousted, or sent to prison or concentration camps, or sometimes killed. Those editors, writers, and performers who remained knew how they were to behave. German culture thus became an obedient tool of Nazi politics.

16. Eugenics

Nazi education and censorship attempted to control people's *minds*. The Nazis also controlled the *bodies* of their citizens as much as possible. Milder controls involved new public-health measures such as an aggressive campaign against smoking: the Nazis banned smoking in certain public places, ran an anti-smoking propaganda campaign, and placed restrictions on how tobacco could be advertised.

Stronger controls extended to the sex and reproductive lives of the citizens, and this takes us into darker territory—the Nazis' embrace of eugenics.

Eugenics was not unique to the Nazi regime or to Germany. As early as 1895, eugenics researcher Adolf Jost had published a book called *The Right to Death*, which called for state control over human reproduction, and many intellectuals in many countries embraced eugenics. In nature, the argument ran, only the strongest males get to mate with the females; the weaker males get to mate less frequently or not at all; this natural selection of the stronger and de-selection of the weaker serves to keep the species healthy and strengthen it.

The same principle holds for farming. Just as a farmer is concerned to improve the quality of his herd, so the state should be concerned to improved the quality of its citizenry. And just as a farmer will not let any bull mate with any cow, so the state should not let just any male have sex with any female; the farmer will select his strongest and healthiest bulls and have them mate only with his strongest, healthiest cows. Those bulls and cows not up to standard are culled from the herd and not allowed to reproduce at all.

As Rudolph Hess, deputy Führer of the Reich, would say a little later: "National Socialism is nothing but applied biology."[34]

Before the Nazis came to power, German intellectuals were among the world leaders in eugenics research. In 1916, Dr. Ernst Rudin, the director of the Genealogical-Demographic Department of the German Institute for Psychiatric Research, established a field of psychiatric hereditary biology based on eugenics theory. Rudin became the president of the International Federation of Eugenic Organizations, the world leader of the eugenics movement. In 1920, psychiatry Professor Alfred Hoche and distinguished jurist Karl Binding wrote *The Permission to Destroy Life Unworthy of Life*. Their book called for the destruction of "worthless" humans for the sake of protecting worthy humans. So-called worthless individuals included the mentally and physically disabled.

Another influential book, *The Principles of Human Heredity and Racial Hygiene*, written by Drs. Eugen Fischer, Lenz, and Bauer, hailed the superiority of the German race and

---

[34] Richard Walther Darré, Reich Minister of Food and Agriculture from 1933 to 1942, had a crucial role intellectually and administratively in determining Nazi policy: "Just as in the animal world, this committed Social Darwinist proposed a system of racial selection in order to 'breed' a new rural nobility and to achieve the 'breeding goal of the German people.' Darré suggested marriage restrictions for Jews and 'less valuable' non-Jews, strict state control of all marriages and fertility, and sterilization of those members of the community who were considered to be a threat to the 'racial purity' of the German people. The Nazis used all of these measures in the subsequent years ..." (Gerhard 2005, pp. 131-132).

called for the use of concentration camps for non-Germans and mixed races. Fischer already had experience with this—having planned and executed the forced sterilization of South Africans who were the offspring of German military men and women indigenous to South Africa.

By the time the Nazis came to power, eugenics was an established part of German intellectual life. One striking indication of this is that German universities had twenty-three official Professors of Racial Hygiene.

National Socialism held that the state should take over where natural selection left off. In line with their collectivism and anti-individualism, the Nazis held that medicine and reproduction should serve the interests of the state rather than the individual. Like the farmer, the Nazis wanted high quality Aryan children for the state's purposes, so they took charge of the mating process of Germany's citizens. The Reich could not allow individuals to rut with just anyone. Taking away individual choice in reproduction would improve the stock and cleanse the nation of bad genetic elements.

The Nazis also argued that they were thus more strongly socialist than their arch-rivals, the Communists. While the Communists focused almost totally on issues of money, capitalism, and economics, the Nazis argued for a more comprehensive socialism: *Every* aspect of human life, including family and reproduction, was to be socialized.

The Nazi eugenics program had two faces: positive and negative.[35] The positive face aimed at increasing the number of pure Aryan births; the negative face aimed at eliminating inferior genetic influences in Germany. In order to implement both sides of the program, the Nazis first needed to define racial purity. They decided that there were three racial categories: *Full Jew*, having three or more Jewish grandparents; two degrees of *Mischlinge*, or mixed types, having either one or two Jewish grandparents; and *Full Aryan*, having no Jewish grand-

---

[35] Using "positive" and "negative" here descriptively, not normatively.

parents. The pure Aryan would be the tall, slender yet strong, blond human being.

This led to some serious parody, given that not many of the Nazi leadership met those criteria. Neither Goebbels nor Göring nor Hitler himself obviously met them.

All humor aside, the Nazis set to achieving the positive face of their program in several ways. They provided incentives to encourage racially pure marriages. Incentives included loans to help married couples get established, subsidies for each child produced and official awards and medals for "hero" mothers of four or more children. Childless couples were vilified. The Nazi government also lowered the age of marriage to sixteen, encouraged the birth of illegitimate Aryan children, outlawed abortion for Aryans, outlawed marriage for sterile women, strictly regulated birth control, and initially forbade mothers from working outside of the home.

Heinrich Himmler was in charge of this area of Nazi policy. Himmler was also the Chief of the SS and the Gestapo, and so was one of the top two or three most powerful Nazis in the regime. Under Himmler's direction, the Nazis also created the *Lebensborn*, or "Fount of Life," program in 1935. This project developed group homes for young, unmarried Aryan women impregnated by Aryan men. Once the racial

Heinrich Himmler

purity of the parents had been established, the young women stayed in the homes and were given free food and medical care. In return, the women signed over all rights to their fetuses, who, upon birth, would be raised by select Nazi families. Between 12,000 and 16,000 infants were born in *Lebensborn* homes in Germany and Nazi-occupied territories. A few years later, in order to speed up the development of a pure Aryan race, the Nazis began to kidnap Aryan children from occupied territories. An estimated 250,000 children six years of age and younger were taken back to Germany and assimilated into Nazi homes.

The negative face of the Nazi's eugenics program required the extermination of non-Aryans. In 1935, the Nazis implemented the Nuremberg Laws for the Protection of Hereditary Health. These laws included forcible sterilization of individuals with mental and hereditary physical defects. During the 1930s, the Nazis sterilized approximately 400,000 people. Certification of Aryan descent became a requirement for marriage; interracial marriages were prohibited; and the remaining rights of Jews were revoked.

The Nazis then introduced extermination. In May of 1935, the regime euthanized twelve patients in a mental hospital in Hadamar, Germany. The Nazi Interior Ministry required that all children under three years of age with congenital malformations and mental deficiencies be registered with the state. Those deemed unfit were taken away from their homes for "special treatment." "Special treatment" meant either being injected with a lethal dose of medicine or simply starved to death. The Nazis were still somewhat cautious about public scrutiny, so part of their strategy was slowly to get the nation accustomed to human extermination before they turned their full attention to the Jews.

The public justification for these deaths was not only the biological health of the state. The Nazis also gave a collectivist economic justification. If the health of the citizenry is the State's responsibility, then the State must allocate its economic resources responsibly. If money and resources are used to care for the weak, then the stronger humans are forced to sacrifice. But the stronger human beings are the State's best assets; it is they who are the realization and the future of the *Volk*. The

State accordingly has a moral obligation not to waste economic resources on the weak; and when the weak are destroyed as nature intended, the strong will be enhanced and the species advanced.

This brings us to Nazi economic policy.

17. Economic controls

Through education and censorship, the Nazis attempted to socialize the German *mind*. Through public health measures and eugenics, they attempted to socialize the German *body*. A natural extension of both policies was to socialize German economic production.

As would be expected by the socialist part of National Socialism, the guiding principle of Nazi economics was that all property belongs to the people, the *Volk*, and was to be used only for the good of the people. Just as one's body is no longer one's private possession but rather belongs to the whole community, economic property was no longer anyone's private possession but to be used by State permission and only for the good of the people.

Upon coming to power, the Nazi government nationalized Jewish property and in 1934 passed a law allowing the expropriation of property owned by communists.

Another early policy given high priority by the Nazi government was the organizing of all German businesses into cartels. The argument was that—in contrast to the disorderliness and egoism of free market capitalism—centralization and state control would increase efficiency and a sense of German unity. In July of 1933, membership in a cartel became compulsory for businesses, and by early 1934 the cartel structure was re-organized and placed firmly under the direction of the German government.

By 1937, small businesses with capital under $40,000 were dissolved by the State; labor unions had been dissolved, as were the rights to strike and collective bargaining. Unemployment was dealt with by public works programs of road-building and so on.

All property and labor power was now either owned by the State or, if still owned by private parties, subject to almost-total control. Businesses were told by the State what to produce and in what quantities. Prices and wages were set by the State.

And if anyone complained, a commonly used Nazi slogan put them on the defensive:[36] "The common interest before self interest." The argument was quite clear: You are not a private individual seeking profit or higher wages in a capitalist economy. You and your property belong in trust to the German people, and you have a duty to serve the public interest, even if it involves a personal sacrifice.

There is an important sub-point worth dwelling upon, for there is a lively debate about just how committed to socialism the Nazis were. After all, they did not outright nationalize all businesses as pure socialism would require; rather they allowed several important businesses to remain in private hands.

A 1935 official statement put the National Socialist policy this way:

> The power economy will not be run by the state, but by (private) entrepreneurs acting under their own free and unrestricted responsibility. ... The state limits itself to the function of control, which is, of course, all-inclusive. It further reserves the right of intervention ... in order to enforce the supremacy of considerations of public interest.[37]

---

[36] "Gemeinnutz geht vor Eigennutz!" (quoted in Meinecke 1950, p. 51); cf. the 1920 Nazi Program.

[37] Quoted in Pipes 1999, p. 221.

The issue about how socialist the Nazis were is, in part, a judgment call about long-term principles and short-term pragmatism.

Here is a related example: Clearly the Nazis were strongly committed to racism. But we could point out that they formed alliances with the Italians and the Japanese, neither of whom are Aryans racially. Yet obviously it would be a mistake to infer from these alliances that the Nazis were not really racist. They *were* racist, but as a matter of short-term strategy and political compromise they were willing to form alliances with those whom they would otherwise despise. Since the Italians and Japanese were powers, it made strategic sense to overlook the racial issue in the short run.[38]

The same holds for the economic socialism: allowing some major businesses to remain officially in private hands made pragmatic economic sense in the short run. The Nazis knew they needed productive businesses to fuel the economy and their developing war machine, so it would have been foolish to interfere too much with smoothly-running enterprises. Additionally, the Nazis knew they could count on the German nationalism of many business owners to go along with what the Nazi government asked of them. And if push came to shove, the Nazis could and did pass precise regulations to direct production as they saw fit.[39]

---

[38] Hitler's pragmatism in foreign policy: "In political life there is no such thing as principles of foreign policy. The programmatic principles of my party are its doctrine on the racial problem and its fight against pacifism and internationalism. But foreign policy is merely a means to an end. In questions of foreign policy I shall never admit that I am tied by anything" (quoted in Heiden, p. xx).

[39] "Buried under mountains of red tape, directed by the State as to what they could produce, how much, and at what price, burdened by increasing taxation and milked by steep and never ending 'special contributions' to the party, the businessmen, who had welcomed Hitler's regime so enthusiastically because they expected it to destroy organized labor and allow an entrepreneur to practice untrammeled free enterprise, became greatly disillusioned.

So while the Nazi government imposed many regulations upon German businesses, the Nazis counted on and received much voluntary commitment and enthusiasm. Most business owners, managers, and workers believed in the cause and devoted their economic energies to it. They saw the personal sacrifices demanded of them as their duty, and they obediently and willingly bore the sacrifices for the good of the cause.

As a result, from 1932 to 1936 Germany underwent an economic boom, lifting itself out of the stagnation of the 1920s and early 1930s. Unemployment fell from six million to one million, national production rose 102% and national income doubled.[40]

By 1936, the same year the Germans hosted the Olympic Games in Berlin, the German economy was again a powerhouse. A national vote was held in March to gauge popular support for Hitler's regime. "Adolf Hitler" was the only name on the ballot, and voters had a choice to vote for Hitler or not. As dubious as the vote was, the numbers do tell us something: 98.6% of the voting population voted, and of those 98.7% voted for Hitler. That means that over 44 million adult Germans expressed approval and only about half a million did not.

18. Militarization

The most important part of the new Germany was the military. On a historically unprecedented scale, the German economy became a war economy.

One of them was Fritz Thyssen, one of the earliest and biggest contributors to the party. Fleeing Germany at the outbreak of the war, he recognized that the 'Nazi regime has ruined German industry.' And to all he met abroad he proclaimed, 'What a fool [*Dummkopf*] I was!'" (Shirer 1962, p. 261).
[40] Shirer 1962, p. 258-259.

Conscription had been re-introduced in 1935, and in 1936 Hermann Göring took over as Germany's economic minister. Under Göring's direction, Germany began to develop a total war economy in earnest. Up until this time, the re-militarization of Germany had been kept semi-secret and had been largely paid for by funds confiscated from enemies of the state and blocked foreign bank accounts.

Hermann Göring

Under Göring's leadership, the re-militarization came out into the open. Göring started a Four Year Plan to make Germany self-sufficient so that it would be able to survive blockades during a war: he reduced imports to a minimum, put price and wage controls in place, built factories to produce rubber, textiles, fuel, and steel—all commodities essential to a war machine—and taxes were increased greatly upon private businesses to fund the war.

Also as promised as long ago as 1920 in the Nazi Party's founding political program, the Nazis initiated a strategy of geographical expansion. In 1936, Germany re-occupied the Rhineland. Also in 1936, Hitler concluded an alliance with Mussolini and Italy and sent troops to Spain to support General Francisco Franco's authoritarian regime. There was no military response from France, England, or the other Allied powers.

In 1938, the Germans took over Austria; no shooting or violence was necessary. After the takeover, a plebiscite was held in which one could vote yes or no for Hitler: In Austria, 99.75% voted for Hitler; in Germany, 99.08% voted for Hitler. Hitler was angry that he received a slightly lower level of support from the Germans than he did from the Austrians. Again there was no military response from the Allies. Instead they believed Hitler was satisfied. They still believed him when he signed the Munich Agreement promising no more expansion beyond the Sudetenland, then a key part of Czechoslovakia. As a result of that agreement, Hitler was named *Time* magazine's Man of the Year for 1938.

Early in 1939, the Germans took over all of Czechoslovakia. Again there was no military response from the Allies.

But on September 1, 1939, the Germans invaded Poland, and this time the Western Allies responded.

World War II had officially begun, and the twentieth century began its second great collision of incompatible philosophies of life—with the broadly liberal, individualistic, democratic, and capitalist Allies of the west at war with the authoritarian, collectivistic, and socialistic Axis powers of the east. And at the end of the war, tens of millions more people would be dead.

The Germans were steeled for war and well prepared physically and psychologically. They believed in *Lebensraum*—in the rightness of Germany's expanding as much as necessary to acquire land and resources to survive. They believed in the rightness of Germany's expanding to re-incorporate ethnic Germans now living in foreign lands. They believed that Germany had a moral mission—even a divine mission—to show the world the way to a brighter, idealistic future and to destroy the tottering and depraved capitalist nations of the West. As Hitler put it at the beginning of the war: "What will be destroyed in this war is a capitalist clique that was and remains willing to annihilate millions of men for the sake of their despicable personal interests."[41]

And of course, the Germans had plans for the Jews.

---

[41] Quoted in Lukacs 1991, p. 121.

19. The Holocaust

In 1821, the German poet Heinrich Heine wrote, "Where books are burnt, in the end people are also burnt." Heine was evoking the terrible era of the Reformation and Counter-Reformation in which both people and books were burned regularly. But he was also making a philosophical point about the importance of ideas: books are about ideas, and ideas matter. We humans live what we believe, and if history teaches us anything it is that people can believe an incredible variety of things about themselves and the world they live in. Books store and transmit ideas, but it is in the minds of actual human beings that ideas live and are put into practice. Burning a book has some stopping power for an idea, but the only way to eliminate an idea fully is to eliminate the individuals who believe it. Dictators know this and they have no compunction about eliminating individuals.

The Nazis were not historically unique in this way—where they were unique is in the huge scale upon which they operated and the cold-bloodedly efficient ruthlessness with which they destroyed, killed, and burned human beings.

Eleven to twelve million human beings were exterminated during the Holocaust; approximately six million of them were Jews. We have all heard the numbers and the terrible stories before, and sometimes it is hard for them not to become just abstract statistics in our minds.

But just think of *one* person you know who lives a real life, has dreams, works hard, loves his or her family, has a quirky sense of humor, wants to travel the world. And then imagine *that* person taken away in the middle of the night, herded into a cattle car, stripped naked, experimented upon without anesthesia, slowly starved, gassed, shoved into an oven and burned to cinders. That is what the Nazis did to millions of human beings.

All of the theoretical ingredients of the National Socialist program that contributed to the Holocaust were announced publicly twenty years before the Holocaust began:

That human beings are divided into collective groups that shape their identity.

That those collective groups are in a life and death competitive struggle with each other.

That any tactic is legitimate in the war of competing groups.

That human beings are not individuals with their own lives to live but are servants of the state.

That the state should have total power over both the minds and bodies of its citizens and may dispose of them as it wishes.

That citizens should obey a higher authority and be willing to make the ultimate sacrifice for the good of their group, as defined by higher authority.

Additionally, during the 1930s the Nazis had experimented with most of the practical techniques that would be used in the Holocaust. In the 1930s, basic human rights to liberty, property, the pursuit of happiness were denied to millions as a matter of official policy. Many of those deemed undesirable had been forced to leave their homes and country. Those who stayed were subject to officially tolerated vandalism, beatings, and occasional murders. Some of those deemed unfit to reproduce had been sterilized. Some of those deemed unfit to live had been euthanized. As early as 1933, concentration camps had been established north of Berlin at Oranienburg and at Dachau in the south of Germany. More camps were added as the decade progressed.

And of course the vicious anti-Semitism of the Nazis and their sympathizers among millions of Germans had been common knowledge and common practice. It is appropriate that the classically-educated Dr. Joseph Goebbels, Reich

Minister of Culture, would express it most bluntly and clearly: "Certainly the Jew is also a Man, but the Flea is also an Animal."[42]

So I return to our early question: How could Nazism happen?

20. The question of Nazism's philosophical roots

We do not do ourselves any favors by not understanding Nazism thoroughly or by being satisfied with superficial explanations. It took a world war to stop National Socialism in the twentieth century. War is brute force. Brute force rarely changes anyone's minds about anything, and it alone does not destroy the underlying causes that motivate conflict. To use a crude analogy: If two neighbors are having an ongoing argument about a series of issues, and one neighbor hits the other and knocks him unconscious—that ends the argument but it does not solve their problems. The source of their argument is still there and it will re-surface.

The same holds for the underlying causes of National Socialism and its differences with the liberal democracies. The liberal democracies were able to knock out the Nazis in World War II, though it was a close call—but the underlying arguments are still with us.

The differences between National Socialism and liberal democracies are profound and involve entirely different philosophies of life. National Socialism was the product of a well-thought-out philosophy of life, the main elements of which were originated, crafted, and argued by philosophers and other intellectuals across many generations.

The Nazi intellectuals were not lightweights, and we run the risk of underestimating our enemy if we dismiss their ideology

---

[42] "Sicher ist der Jude auch ein Mann, aber der Floh ist auch ein Tier."

as attractive only to a few cranky weirdos.[43] If your enemy has a machine gun but you believe he only has a pea shooter, then you are setting yourself up for failure. And if we remind ourselves of the list of very heavyweight intellectuals who supported Nazism—Nobel Prize winners, outstanding philosophers and brilliant legal thinkers—then it is clear that these were no pea-shooters and that we need heavyweight intellectual ammunition to defend ourselves.

In the case of other major historical revolutions, we are more familiar with seeing the significance of philosophy. When we think for example of the causes of the Communist Revolutions in Russia and China, we naturally think back to the philosopher Karl Marx. When we think of the causes of the French Revolution, we think back to Jean-Jacques Rousseau. When we think of the causes of the American Revolution, we naturally think back to

Karl Marx

the philosopher John Locke. The same holds the causes of National Socialism—although since the Nazi regime went so horribly wrong, there is perhaps some reluctance to name names. Yet naming names is sometimes crucial if we are going to get to the historical heart of the matter. What philosophers can we cite in the case of the Nazis? Several names are candidates: Georg Hegel, Johann Fichte, even elements from Karl Marx.

But in connection with the Nazis, perhaps the biggest and the most controversial name regularly mentioned is that of Friedrich Nietzsche. The Nazis often cited Nietzsche as one of their philosophical precursors, and even though Nietzsche died thirty-three years before the Nazis came to power, references to Nietzsche crop up regularly in Nazi writings and activities.

---

[43] Recall Albert Speer on "the event that led me to [Hitler]"—a speech Hitler gave to the College of Engineering in Berlin: Speer expected it to be "a bombastic harangue" but it turned out to be a "reasoned lecture" (quoted in Orlow 1969, p. 199).

In philosopher Heidegger's lectures, for example, "Nietzsche was presented as *the* Nazi philosopher."[44]

In his study, Adolf Hitler had a bust of Friedrich Nietzsche. In 1935, Hitler attended and participated in the funeral of Nietzsche's sister Elisabeth. In 1938, the Nazis built a monument to Nietzsche. In 1943, Hitler gave a set of Nietzsche's writings as a gift to fellow dictator Benito Mussolini.[45]

Hitler's propaganda minister, Joseph Goebbels, was also a great admirer of Friedrich Nietzsche. In his semi-autobiographical novel, Goebbels has the title character Michael die in a mining accident—afterward three books are found among his belongings: the Bible, Goethe's *Faust*, and Nietzsche's *Thus Spake Zarathustra*.

So who was Friedrich Nietzsche?

---

[44] Rohkrämer 2005, p. 181.

[45] During WWI, the German government printed 150,000 copies of Nietzsche's *Thus Spake Zarathustra* and gave them to soldiers along with a copy of the Bible.

Part 5. Nietzsche's Life and Influence

21. Who was Friedrich Nietzsche?

"That which does not kill us makes us stronger." "Live *dangerously!*"[46]

Friedrich Nietzsche was a nineteenth-century German philosopher famous for his worship of human potential and for encouraging individuals to seek great heights and make real their creative dreams. He is also famous for his absolute loathing of all things small, cowardly, or mediocre.

In his writings we find a corresponding reverence of all things

Friedrich Nietzsche

great, noble, heroic. He spoke directly and passionately to the best within each of us: "Do not throw away the hero in your soul" and "Hold holy your highest hope."[47] And for those of us who sense we have a creative spark that must be honored and nurtured—"the noble soul has reverence for itself."[48]

One indication of the importance of Nietzsche is the pantheon of major twentieth century intellectuals whom he influenced.

He was an influence on Jean-Paul Sartre and Hermann Hesse, major writers, both of whom won Nobel Prizes. He

---

[46] *EH* "Why I Am So Wise" 2 and GS 283.
[47] *Z* I.
[48] *BGE* 287.

was an influence on thinkers as diverse in their outlooks as
Ayn Rand and Michel Foucault. Rand's politics are classically
liberal—while Foucault's are far Left, including a stint as a
member of the French Communist Party. There is the striking fact that Nietzsche was an atheist, but he was an influence
on Martin Buber, one of the most widely-read theologians of
the twentieth century. And Nietzsche said harsh things about
the Jews, as we will see—but he was nonetheless admired by
Chaim Weizmann, a leader of the Zionist movement and first
president of Israel.

So what is the attraction of Nietzsche? There is the ex-
citing, sometimes scorching prose—Nietzsche was a stylist *par
excellence*. There is his romanticism of life as a great, daring adventure. And of importance to serious intellectuals, there is the
fundamentality and sheer audacity of the questions he raises
about the human condition.

According to his teachers and professors, the young
Friedrich Nietzsche showed extraordinary intellectual promise.
He was appointed professor at University of Basel in Switzer-
land—at the age of twenty-four, which is unusually young for
a professor. Even more unusually, he was appointed before fin-
ishing his doctoral degree, which was almost unheard of.

As brilliant as Nietzsche was, he was not suited for academic life. By most accounts he was a terrible lecturer, and he
suffered from chronic health problems, which contributed to a
general nervous collapse in 1870.

From the late 1870s, he wandered mostly alone and
lonely over Europe, surveying the cultural landscape.

And when we take stock of the world in the late nineteenth century, what do we learn?

22. God is dead

"God is dead." For thousands of years we have believed in religion. But in the modern world religion has become a shadow
of its former self. Nietzsche's dramatic phrase, *God is dead*, is
meant to capture the personal and shocking quality of this rev-
elation.[49] For those of us raised religiously, religion personal-
ized the world. It gave us a sense that the world has a purpose
and that we are part of a larger plan. It gave us a comfort that,
despite appearances, we are all equal and cared for and that
upon death—instead of a cold grave—a happily-ever-after ending awaits us.

We find that hard to believe anymore. In the modern
world we have seen the dramatic rise of science providing different, less comfortable answers to questions religion tradition-
ally had a monopoly on. We have thrown off the shackles of
feudalism with its unquestioning acceptance of authority and
knowing our place. We are more individualistic and naturalis-
tic in our thinking.[50]

But in historical time, all of this has happened very
quickly—in the span of a few centuries.

For millennia we have been religious, but come the
nineteenth century even the average man has heard that religion may have reached the end of its road. For most of us, even
the suggestion of this hints at a crisis.

Imagine a thirteen-year old who is awakened in the
middle of the night to be told by strangers that his parents have
died. He is suddenly an orphan. As long as he can remember,
his mother and father have been presences in his life, looking after him and guiding him, sometimes firmly, but always
a benevolent protection and support in a world that he is not
yet able to handle on his own. Now they are gone and, ready
or not, he is thrust into that world alone. How does the young

---

[49] GS 108, 125.
[50] GS 117.

teen handle that sudden transition?

Culturally, Nietzsche believes, we are like that young teen. For as long as we can remember, our society has relied on God the Father to look after us—to be a benevolent and sometimes stern guiding force through a difficult world. But suddenly we are orphaned: we wake up one morning to discover in our heart of hearts that our naïvely childhood religious beliefs have withered.

So now, whether we like it or not, a question creeps into our minds: How do we face the prospect of a world without God and religion?

Well, says Nietzsche, in the nineteenth century most people do *not* face that question well.

23. Nihilism's symptoms

Most people avoid the issue, sensing that even to raise it would be to enter dangerous territory. They sense that the game might be up for religion, but out of fear they shutter their minds and will themselves to believe that God is still out there somewhere. Life without religion is too scary to contemplate, so they retreat to a safety zone of belief and repeat nervously the formulas they have learned about faith. Now, believes Nietzsche, it is one thing for a medieval peasant to have a simple-minded faith, but for us moderns such a faith has a tinge of dishonesty about it.

Slightly better to Nietzsche, but not much, are the socialists of the nineteenth century.[51] Socialism is on the rise, and many socialists have abandoned the religion of their youth—but only halfway. Most socialists accept that God is dead—but then they are very concerned that the State take God's place and look after them. The mighty State will provide for us and tell us what to do and protect us against the mean people of the world.

---

[51] *Z* 1:11; *TI* Skirmishes 34; also 37: "Socialists are decadents." See also *HAH* 473: "Socialism is the fanciful younger brother of the almost expired despotism whose heir it wants to be."

Think of it this way: The Judeo-Christian tradition says this is a world of sin, in which the weak suffer at the hands of the strong; that we should all be selfless and serve God and others, especially the sick and helpless; and that in a future ideal world—heaven—the lion will lay down with lamb, and the inescapable power of God will bring salvation to the meek and judgment to the wicked.

The Marxist socialist tradition says this is a world of evil exploitation, in which the strong take advantage of the weak. But we should all be selfless and sacrifice for the good of others, especially the needy—"From each according to his ability, to each according to his need"—and that the forces of history will necessarily bring about a future ideal world ending all harsh competition, empowering the oppressed and eliminating the evil exploiters.

Both religion and socialism thus glorify weakness and need. Both recoil from the world as it is: tough, unequal, harsh. Both flee to an imaginary future realm where they can feel safe. Both say to you: Be a nice boy. Be a good little girl. Share. Feel sorry for the little people. And both desperately seek someone to look after them—whether it be God or the State.

And where, asks Nietzsche, are the men of courage? Who is willing to stare into the abyss? Who can stand alone on the icy mountaintop? Who can look a tiger in the eye without flinching?

Such men exist. Every generation produces its occasional magnificent men—sparkling, vital individuals who accept easily that life is tough, unequal, unfair, and who welcome asserting their

Wanderer Above the Sea of Fog, **Caspar Friedrich, 1818**

strength to meet the challenge. Those who have unbending wills against anything the world can throw at them.

But such magnificent human beings are few and far between in the nineteenth century, and Nietzsche wonders why. And he looks back on past cultures where the magnificent men dominated: strength was prized and inequality was a fact of life. Assertiveness and conquest were a source of pride. He names the Japanese feudal nobility as an example, with their samurai code of honor, and the Indian Brahmins who rose and imposed their caste system, the Vikings who raided ruthlessly up and down the European coast, the expansionist Arabs—and of course the awesome Roman Empire.[52]

What explains this stark contrast? Why do some cultures rise to greatness and unabashedly impose their will upon the world—while other cultures seem apologetic and urge upon us a bland conformity?

24. Masters and slaves

Part of the answer, says Nietzsche, is biological.

All of organic nature is divided into two broad species-types—those animals that are naturally herd animals and those that are naturally loners—those that are prey and those that are predators. Some animals are by nature sheep, field mice, or cows—and some animals are by nature wolves, hawks, or lions. Psychologically and physically, this divide also runs right through the human species. Some people are born fearful and inclined to join a herd—and some are born fearless and inclined to seek lonely heights. Some are born sedentary and sluggish—and some are born crackling with purpose and craving adventure.[53] Some of us, to use Nietzsche's language, are born to be slaves, and some are born to be masters.

And which type you are—there is little you can do about it. There is a brute biological fact here: Each of us is the

[52] *GM*, 1:11.
[53] *TI* "Skirmishes" 33, 35.

product of a long line of evolution, and our traits are evolutionarily bred into us. Just as a sheep cannot help but be sheepish
and a hawk cannot help but be hawkish, each of us inherits
from our parents and from their parents before them a long line
of inbuilt traits. "It cannot be erased from a man's soul what
his ancestors have preferably and most constantly done."[54]

The master types live by strength, creativity, independence, assertiveness, and related traits. They respect power,
courage, boldness, risk-taking, even recklessness. It is natural
for them to follow their own path no matter what, to rebel
against social pressure and conformity.[55]

The slave types live in conformity. They tend to pas-
sivity, dependence, meekness. It is natural for them to stick
together for a sense of security, just as herd animals do.[56]

Now, Nietzsche says, let's talk about *morality*, about
good and bad, right and wrong. For a long time we have been
taught that morality is a matter of religious commandments set
in stone thousands of years ago.

Not so, says Nietzsche. What we take to be moral
depends on our biological nature—and different biological natures dictate different moral codes.

Think of it this way: If you are a sheep, then what will
seem good to you as a sheep? Being able to graze peacefully,
sticking close together with others just like you, being part
of the herd and not straying off. What will seem bad to you?
Well, wolves will seem bad, and anything wolf-like, predatory,
aggressive. But what if you are a wolf? Then strength, vicious-
ness, and contempt for the sheep will come naturally to you
and seem good. There is nothing the wolves and the sheep can
agree on morally—their natures are different, as are their needs
and goals, as is what feels good to them. Of course it would be
good for the sheep if they could convince the wolves to be more
sheep-like—but what self-respecting wolf would fall for that?

[54] *BGE* 264.
[55] *GM* 1:6.
[56] *BGE* 199.

That lambs dislike great birds of prey does not seem strange: only it gives no grounds for reproaching these birds of prey for bearing off little lambs. And if the lambs say among themselves: 'these birds of prey are evil; and whoever is least like a bird of prey, but rather its opposite, a lamb—would he not be good?' there is no reason to find fault with this institution of an ideal, except perhaps that the birds of prey might view it a little ironically and say: 'we don't dislike them at all, these good little lambs; we even love them: nothing is more tasty than a tender lamb.'[57]

The same point holds for humans. The divide between strong and weak, assertive and timid, runs straight through the human species. The key question to ask about morality is *not*: Is such and such a value universally and intrinsically good? Rather the question is: *What kind of person* finds this value to be valuable?

In Nietzsche's words, one's moral code is a "decisive witness to who he is," to the "innermost drives of his nature."[58] "Moral judgments," Nietzsche says, are "symptoms and sign languages which betray the process of physiological prosperity or failure."[59]

So: one's moral code is a function of one's psychological make-up, and one's psychological make-up is a function of one's biological make-up.

The biological language and examples in those quotations show that biology is crucial to Nietzsche's views on morality. Nietzsche was a precocious fifteen years old when

---

[57] *GM* 1:13.
[58] *BGE* 6.
[59] *WP* 258. See also *D* 542 and *BGE* 221.

Charles Darwin's book *On the Ori-gin of Species* was published in 1859. Evolutionary ideas had been in the air for a long time before Darwin, and much of the intellectual world was moving away from thinking of the reality in terms of timeless, un-changing absolutes to viewing it in terms of process and change. All of this applies to morality too.

Charles Darwin

Moral codes, Nietzsche is here suggesting, are part of a biological type's life strategy of survival, and the more we look at the history of morality evolutionarily and biologically, the more we are struck by the diversity of circumstances and how dramatically beliefs about values have changed across time.

This is precisely our key problem culturally, Nietzsche argues. The evidence shows that we once prized excellence and power and looked down upon the humble and the lowly. Now the meek, the common man, the kindly neighbor are the "good guys" while the aggressive, the powerful, the strong, the proud are "evil."[60]

Think of it this way: Suppose I gave you the following list of traits and urged them upon you positively.

It is good to be *proud* of yourself, to have a healthy sense of *self-esteem*.

Wealth is good, for it gives you the power to live as you wish.

Be *ambitious* and *bold*, and seek your highest dream.

Don't take any nonsense from other people—make it clear that you will take *vengeance* and exact *justice* against those who mess with you.

---

[60] *GM* 1:4.

Seek to improve your life and devote yourself only to things that will *profit* you; don't waste your time or resources.

Seek great *challenges*, great *pleasures*, including *sensual* pleasures of the body, and go your own *independent* way in life, embracing whatever *risks* you must to develop a full and realized sense of yourself as an *individual*.

And when you accomplish something great, *admire yourself* for what you have done and *indulge* yourself in the rewards that greatness deserves.

Pride, Self-esteem

Wealth

Ambition, Boldness

Vengeance

Justice

Profit

Challenge

Pleasure, Sensuality

Independence

Risk

Individualism

Admiration of self

Indulgence

Now consider the elements in this list together as a package. Does that list resonate with you? Do you feel in your bones that if more people lived this way they would live more active, fuller lives and they and the human species would realize its highest potential?

Now consider a different list of traits, and let me urge them upon you positively too.

One should be *humble*, for *pride goeth before the fall*. The *meek* shall inherit the earth, and blessed are the *poor*. As for wealth and the rich, *it shall be easier for a camel to pass through the eye of a needle than for a rich man to get into heaven*. Instead of seeking profit, one should *sacrifice* and give to *charity*. Be *patient* and *forgiving*. *Turn the other cheek*. Be aware of one's *weaknesses* and *sins*, and be *ashamed* and self-deprecating as a result. Practice *self-restraint*, particularly with respect to your lower, impure, and often *disgusting physical* desires. Play it *safe*, think of other people's needs and *don't rock the boat*, and realize that we're all *dependent* upon each other. *Obey* your parents and your preacher and the politicians.

El Greco, *Laocoön*, c. 1610/1614

Masters	*Slaves*
Pride, Self-esteem	Humility; Pride goeth before the fall.
Bold	The meek shall inherit the earth.
Rich	Blessed are the poor.
Wealth	It shall be easier for a camel to pass through the eye of the needle than for a rich man to get into heaven.
Profit	Sacrifice, Charity
Ambition	Patience
Vengeance	Forgiveness
Justice	Turn the other cheek
Sense of self worth	Weakness, sinfulness
Admiration of self	Shame
Indulgence	Self-restraint
Sensuality	Disgust at the physical
Challenge	Safety
Individualism	Don't rock the boat
Independence	Dependence
Autonomy	Obedience

Does the list on the right resonate with you? Do you feel that if more people lived that way they would live better lives and they and the human species would realize its highest potential?

Nietzsche is crystal clear about the list on the right—that list is *dangerous* to human potential. It reeks of weakness, even sickness and unhealthiness. It undermines the human potential for greatness, and it is, tragically, the dominant morality of our time. In our time, the traits that ennoble man are condemned, and all the traits that weaken man are praised. Morality, as Nietzsche puts it paradoxically, has become a bad thing;

morality has become immoral: "precisely morality would be to blame if the highest power and splendor actually possible to the type man was never in fact attained? So that precisely morality was the danger of dangers?"[61]

Accordingly, Nietzsche concludes, "we need a critique of moral values, the value of these values themselves must first be called in question—and for that there is needed a knowledge of the conditions and circumstances in which they grew, under which they evolved and changed."[62]

25. The origin of slave morality

Our problem is this: Somehow the morality of the weak has become dominant, and the morality of the strong has declined. How is this rather paradoxical state of affairs to be explained?

Part of the story depends on our individual biological and psychological make-ups—for each of us individually, one or the other of the two moralities resonates more within us. But part of the story is cultural, because sometimes the master morality dominates a culture and sometimes the slave morality dominates—and here there is a history lesson.[63]

Part of the historical story is that the modern world has embraced democracy, and democracy means giving power to the majority, and a majority of people are, shall we say, conformist in their tastes, concerned with what their neighbors think about them, looking forward to retirement when they won't have to do anything, content to sit passively in their little homes gossiping and griping about their bosses and mothers-in-law.

Democracy gives *that* sort of person power, so we should expect that democratic laws and policies will reflect the tastes and interests of that sort of person. Democracies tailor their policies to the majority—not to the exceptional few who

---

[61] *GM* Preface 6.
[62] *GM* Preface 6.
[63] *GM* Preface 3 and 6.

are radicals, trailblazers, and uncompromising risk-takers.

But according to Nietzsche, the modern movement to democracy is itself an effect of deeper historical causes. If we reflect again on the elements that were on the right side of the list—*Pride goeth before the fall*; *Blessed are the meek*; *Turn the other cheek*—clearly all of them come out of the Western religious traditions.

Nietzsche is forthrightly blaming the Judeo-Christian moral tradition for the rise of the slave morality.[64] For Nietzsche, there are no essential differences between Judaism and Christianity—Jesus was a Jew who wanted to reform Judaism, and the ensuing split between Judaism and Christianity is a matter of two variations on the same theme.  Both Judaism and Christianity share the same roots and the same general approach to morality. Nietzsche traces the origin of that morality back to a decisive set of events early in Jewish history, before the time of Moses. That event was the enslavement of the Jews in Egypt. If we recall our Biblical history, the Jews were for a long time a slave people under powerful Egyptian masters.

Yet we know that the Jews found a way to survive their enslavement under the Egyptians, and while their Egyptian masters have long since perished the Jews have survived, spread across the globe, and they have kept their religion and culture alive despite often horrible adversity. How did the Jews do it?

Here Nietzsche says the Jews asked themselves some very realistic, practical questions about morality. If it is good to survive, then what policies and actions will keep you alive? And if you happen to be a slave, how does one survive as a slave? And, by contrast, what policies and actions will likely get

---

[64] *GM* 1:7.

you killed? If you are a slave and you have children whom you desperately want to survive and grow up, what will you teach your slave children to increase their chances of doing so?

Here Nietzsche is saying that what is good and bad, what is moral and immoral, is not a matter of supernatural theological commandments that hold for all circumstances timelessly. What is good and bad is a matter of real-life, practical circumstances, and different circumstances call for different moral strategies.

So if your real-life circumstance is that you are a slave, what strategy will be moral—that is, what strategy will actually help you survive?

Clearly, if you are going to survive as a slave, then you must obey the master. This does not come naturally. All living things, says Nietzsche, have an instinct to express themselves, to assert their power. So as a slave you have to stifle your natural instinct. Or suppose the master strikes you because you did something wrong—the desire for revenge comes naturally—but you have to stifle it. You train yourself to restrain your natural impulses and to internalize a humble, patient, obedient self. The slaves who don't do this end up dead. Slaves who are proud, impatient, and disobedient do not last long. Consequently, slave virtues of obedience and humility have survival value. And those are the traits you will drill into your children if you want them to survive. Slave virtues thus become cultural values across generations. Thus, Nietzsche argues, during this decisive event in early Jewish history, the slave values became the internalized cultural values of the Jews.[65]

Notice that Nietzsche is saying that obedience, humility, forgiveness, and patience are moral *not* because some supernatural being commanded them to be so—fundamentally, morality has nothing to do with religion. The goodness of those traits is based on down-to-earth, nitty-gritty, practical

---

[65] *GM* 1:14.

how-do-you-survive-in-a-tough-world-of-power-struggles considerations. If you are a slave in such a world, then slave morality is a tool of survival.

Now of course time passes and many people forget where their culture's moral code came from. Or they are passive and don't think much about it at all and simply accept the prevailing norms. And even among the slaves many are sheep-like and do not especially mind being slaves. But others resent it. And here the story Nietzsche tells becomes darker.

Some of those Jews who are slaves under the Egyptians and later masters are living human beings with a human being's desire to live, grow, express who one is. But they cannot express it. To live as a slave is to be frustrated constantly, and the more one is energetic and alive, the greater one's frustration.[66]

Such slaves will naturally start to resent the master strongly—and they will also start to hate themselves for having to do what the master says. How do you feel when the boss tells you to do something you don't want to do? Do you tell the boss to take this job and shove it—or do you knuckle under silently and do what he says all the while resenting it? And if you knuckle under often enough and resent long enough, what does that do to your soul? The pressure builds up: Not only do you start to hate the master, you start to hate yourself for being such a weakling and knuckling under. And that in turn causes unbearable pressure inside, psychologically. And that is when psychologically ugly things start to happen.

Nietzsche puts the point this way: "The outward discharge was inhibited [and] turned backward against man himself. Hostility, cruelty, joy in persecuting, in attacking, in change, in destruction—all this turned against the possessors of such instincts: that is the origin of the 'bad conscience.'"[67]

---

[66] *GM* 2:10.

[67] *GM* 1:16. Also: "but to think revenge without possessing the force and courage to carry it out, means to carry about a chronic suffering, a poisoning of body and soul" (*HH* 1.60).

So if you are one of those who have this bad conscience, how do you console yourself? How do you *not* descend into self-destructive rage? How do you channel all that pent-up energy and frustration in a safe direction that nonetheless lets you feel good about yourself? You cannot take *real* revenge against the masters—but what about *fantasy* revenge?

Here Nietzsche asks us to think about priests, those who are not the usual sheep-like followers of a religion but who are cleverer, who are more driven and ambitious, and who feel more acutely the internal battle between the natural animal drive for power and the demands of a morality that has taught them to be selfless and humble. Inside such priests, Nietzsche says, we find the most interesting and disturbing psychological phenomena.

Nietzsche puts it harshly: "It is because of their impotence that in them hatred grows to monstrous and uncanny proportions. The truly great haters in world history have always been priests."[68]

And what are the priests of the Judeo-Christian tradition constantly talking about in their sermons? Isn't it one big revenge fantasy?

They tell their flocks that it is good to be humble, meek, and obedient. But to whom is one to be obedient? Well, to God of course. But God is not often around, so being obedient to God in practical terms means being obedient to God's representatives here on earth—and guess who those people are. Of course, it is the priests. So this is part of the strategy: form a power base of large numbers of people who are your obedient followers. You might not have quality people on your side, but sometimes large quantities of people can be a powerful weapon.

Another part of the sermon is to condemn those who are rich, powerful, and assertive—to demand of them that they give away their money, put their power in the service of the weak and the sick, and be like the lion that is supposed to

_____
[68] *GM* 1:7.

lie down with the lamb and not eat it for lunch. What is the point of all these sermons against the rich and the powerful? Of course part of it is a consolation for those in your audience who are weak and poor—it plays on their envy of the rich and powerful and gives them the satisfaction of hearing the rich and the powerful getting a tongue-lashing.

But the sermon is also meant as a direct weapon against the rich and the powerful and is meant to induce in them a sense of guilt and self-doubt about who they are and how they live. The moral sermons are psychological weapons in the battle of the weak against the strong, and the weak use *psychological* weapons since *physical* weapons are not their forte. The priests never use physical confrontation against the masters, and the masters find it beneath their dignity to fight against an unarmed, and to them contemptible, enemy. Instead the priests use *morality* as their weapon of confrontation: they praise the meek and condemn the strong. Judeo-Christian ethics, Nietzsche says, "has waged deadly war against this higher type of man; it has placed all the basic instincts of his type under ban."[69]

The Judeo-Christian moral code, Nietzsche concludes, becomes part of their revenge strategy. Its point is to enable the weaker to survive in a harsh world in which they are often on the receiving end of the big stick—but also to undermine the master-type's confidence in themselves and eventually to subdue and bring down the masters so as to exact a spiritual revenge.[70]

As evidence of this, Nietzsche reminds us of standard Judeo-Christian rhetoric about how, despite current appearances, the weak, the sick, and the poor will triumph in the end. Their kingdom shall come some day and God will visit his wrath upon the rich and powerful. In a perfect catch, Ni-

---

[69] *A* 5.
[70] *BGE* 219; *GM* 1:7, 1:10, 1:15.

etzsche quotes St. Thomas Aquinas, the patron saint of Catholic theology and the most influential philosopher of Christianity for the last millennium: "In order that the bliss of the saints may be more delightful for them and that they may render more copious thanks to God for it, it is given to them to see perfectly the punishment of the damned."[71]

St. Thomas Aquinas

Boiling all of this down to two essential points, Nietzsche believes that the slave morality of the Judeo-Christian tradition is a two-fold strategy: (1) it is a survival code that enables the weak to band together for survival; and (2) it is as revenge and a power play in their battle against the strong.

In Nietzsche's judgment there is no serious question about who is winning the age-old battle.

An early Christian Church father named Tertullian once asked, rhetorically: "What has Athens to do with Jerusalem?" In early church history, Christians such as Tertullian were regularly argued with and mocked by philosophers of the pagan schools of classical Greek philosophy. The point of Tertullian's reply—"What has Athens to do with Jerusalem?"—was that the traditions that came out of Athens and the traditions that came out of Jerusalem are opposed and have nothing to do with one another. It is an age-old battle for dominance over the soul of the Western world.

Nietzsche agrees, but he phrases the point differently. Jerusalem is the home of the major Western religious traditions, all of them stemming from Judaism. But instead of Athens, Nietzsche points to classical Rome as the greatest height

---

[71] *GM* 1:15n. Aquinas, *Summa Theologiae*. III, Supplementum, Q.94, A.1 and 3: "Whether the blessed in heaven will see the sufferings of the damned?" and "Whether the blessed rejoice in the punishment of the wicked?" In Article 3, Aquinas qualifies the rejoicing by stating that it is in reaction to the justice of God's punishment of the wicked.

the pagan traditions achieved. In Rome, the philosophy and art of the Greeks was combined with the political and military genius of the Romans to create the greatest empire the world had ever seen.[72]

So in Nietzsche's reading of history, the great battle for the soul of the Western world is: *Rome versus Judea.*

As evidence of whether Rome or Judea is winning, he invites us to consider to whom one kneels down before in Rome today. The Judeo-Christians have taken over Rome, and to use Nietzsche's words, "everything is visibly becoming Judaized, Christian-ized, mob-ized."[73] The chief slave has for a long time established his camp and planted his flag in the center of what was the greatest master empire the world had ever seen.

All of this is a great moral crisis, and it is a crisis because the future development of mankind is at stake. What kind of species do we want to be? In what way do we want to develop? The moral code we choose will set our course. What most people consider to be the only morality possible, Judeo-Christian morality, Nietzsche sees as a threat to human development because it damns all those traits of assertiveness and egoism and independence and risk-taking that make human greatness and development possible—and that same morality praises smallness and meekness and falling on your knees in shame—all traits that undermine human greatness.

"Nothing stands more malignantly in the way of [mankind's] rise and evolution ... than what in Europe today is called simply 'morality.'" And more bluntly: "let me declare expressly that in the days when mankind was not yet ashamed of its cruelty, life on earth was more cheerful than it is now."[74]

So the current dominance of the Judeo-Christian mo-

---

[72] Nietzsche: "For the Romans were the strong and the noble, and nobody stronger and nobler has yet existed on earth or even been dreamed of" (*GM* 1.16).

[73] *GM* 1:9.

[74] *GM* 2:7.

rality is an unhealthy development that must be overcome.[75] The fate of the human species depends upon it. We must go beyond good and evil.

26. The overman

Nietzsche once said that he philosophized with a hammer.[76] By that he did not mean anything crude like a sledgehammer that smashes things. He had in mind a delicate hammer like the one a piano tuner uses to strike keys on a finely-built musical instrument—to see which notes ring clear and which are discordant or muddy. In writing his philosophy, Nietzsche intended for his words to be like that delicate hammer on your soul. When you read them, how does your soul respond? Does it vibrate clearly—or does it wobble uncertainly? When you hear that God is dead—do those words cause you to shrink inside and fill with a squishy panic—or do they strike a clear, pure, liberating note that heralds the beginning of the tremendous symphony that you can become?

God is dead, so we must become gods and create our own values. Yet most people are afraid of legislating for themselves. They know there is inequality and risk out there in the big, bad world. So they want to let some higher power shoulder the responsibility. But, Nietzsche says, for some precious few among us, the realization that God is dead galvanizes every fiber of their being. They respond by feeling, both passionately and solemnly: *I* will become the author. *I* will create. *I* will embrace the responsibility—*joyously*. *I* will move beyond good and evil and create a new, magnificent set of values.

Such an individual will raise mankind to a higher level of existence. He will be on the path to the *Übermensch*—the superman or overman.

---

[75] Noting here that toward the end of *The Will to Power*, Nietzsche argues that the new masters will thus combine the physical vitality of the aristocratic masters with the spiritual ruthlessness of the slave-priests of Christianity: the new masters will be "Caesars with the soul of Christ" (*WP* 983).
[76] Preface to *Ecce Homo*.

The entire history of mankind, Nietzsche believes, will have prepared the *Übermensch* for his great creative adventure. In himself he will embody the best of the past. The physical vitality and exuberance of the past master types will flow through his veins. But Nietzsche also credits the Judeo-Christian tradition for its internalized, spiritual development—by turning all of its energy inward and stressing ruthless self-discipline and self-denial, that tradition has been a vehicle for the development of a stronger, more capable type of spirit. The new masters will thus combine the physical vitality of the aristocratic masters with the spiritual ruthlessness of the slave-priests of Christianity. As Nietzsche put it in a memorable phrase, the new masters will be "Caesars with the soul of Christ."[77]

Napoleon on his Imperial Throne, **Jean Auguste Dominique Ingres (1806)**

We cannot say ahead of time what new values the masters will create. Not being *Übermenschen* ourselves, we do not have the power to decide for them or even predict. But Nietzsche does indicate strongly what broad direction the new masters will take.

(1) The overman will find his deepest instinct and let it be a tyrant. The creative source of the future lies in *instinct, passion*, and *will*. To put the point negatively, the overman will not rely much on reason. Reason of course is the favorite method of modern, scientific man, but Nietzsche holds that reason is an artificial tool of weaklings—those who need to feel safe and secure build fantasy orderly structures for themselves. Instead, instincts are the deepest parts of your nature—and to the ex-

---

[77] *WP* 983.

tent that you feel a powerful instinct welling up within you, you should nurture it and let it dominate—for from that spring flows true creativity and true exaltation.

> One thing is needful—To 'give style' to one's character—a great and rare art! ... . In the end, when the work is finished, it becomes evident how the constraint of a single taste governed and formed everything large and small. Wheth-er this taste was good or bad is less important than one might suppose, if only it was a single taste![78]

And again: The "'great man' is great owing to the free play and scope of his desires and to the yet greater power that knows how to press these magnificent monsters into service."[79]

(2) Another hint Nietzsche gives us is that the overman will face conflict and exploitation easily, as a fact of life, and he will enter the fray eagerly. In the face of conflict many people become squeamish and given to wishing that life could be kinder and gentler. For such people, Nietzsche has nothing but contempt: "people now rave everywhere, even under the guise of science, about coming conditions of society in which 'the exploiting character' is to be absent:—that sounds to my ear as if they promised to invent a mode of life which should refrain from all organic functions."[80]

Conflict and exploitation are built into life, and the overman himself will not only accept that as natural but will himself be a master of conflict and exploitation.

As Nietzsche puts it, "We think that ... everything evil, terrible, tyrannical in man, everything in him that is kin to beasts of prey and serpents, serves the enhancement of the species 'man' as much as its opposite does."[81]

And further: "a higher and more fundamental value

---

[78] *GS* 290.
[79] *WP* 933.
[80] *BGE* 259.
[81] *BGE* 44.

for life might have to be ascribed to deception, selfishness, and lust."[82]

(3) Another suggestion Nietzsche gives us is this: The overman will naturally accept the fact of great inequalities among men and the fact of his own superiority. The overman will have no qualms about his superior abilities—and his superior *worth* to all others.

About the superior men, Nietzsche forthrightly proclaims: "Their right to exist, the privilege of the full-toned bell over the false and cracked, is a thousand times greater: they alone are our warranty for the future, they alone are liable for the future of man."[83]

So those who are strong should revel in their superiority and ruthlessly impose their wills upon everyone else, just as the masters did in past aristocratic societies. "Every enhancement of the type 'man' has so far been the work of an aristocratic society—and it will be so again and again—a society that believes in the long order of rank and differences in value between man and man, and that needs slavery in some sense or other."[84]

(4) And, as the last quotation suggests, Nietzsche indicates approvingly that the overman will have no problem with using and exploiting others ruthlessly to achieve his ends. "Mankind in the mass sacrificed to the prosperity of a single stronger species of man—that would be an advance."[85]

Nietzsche gives a name to his anticipated overman: He calls him *Zarathustra*, and he names his greatest literary and philosophical work in his honor.

Zarathustra will be the creative tyrant. Having mas-

---

[82] *BGE* 2.
[83] *GM* 3:14.
[84] *BGE* 257.
[85] *GM* 2:12.

tered himself and others, he will exuberantly and energetically command and realize a magnificent new reality. Zarathustra will lead mankind beyond themselves and into an open-ended future.

Nietzsche longs for Zarathustra's coming. "But some day, in a stronger age than this decaying, self-doubting present, he must yet come to us, the redeeming man of great love and contempt ... This man of the future, who will redeem us not only from the hitherto reigning ideal but also from that which was bound to grow out of it, the great nausea, the will to nothingness, nihilism; ... this Antichrist and antinihilist; this victor over God and nothingness—he must come one day.—"[86]

And on that prophetic note, Friedrich Nietzsche stops—and leaves the future in our hands.

---

[86] *GM* 2:24.

Part 6. Nietzsche against the Nazis

27. Five differences

Now we can ask the big pay-off question. After surveying National Socialist theory and practice and engaging with Friedrich Nietzsche's philosophy, we can ask: How much do Nietzsche and the Nazis have in common? Or to put it another way: To what extent were the Nazis justified in seeing Nietzsche as a precursor of their movement?

We know that Adolf Hitler, Joseph Goebbels, and most of the major intellectuals of National Socialism were admirers of Nietzsche's philosophy. They read him avidly during their formative years, recommended him to their peers, and incorporated themes and sayings from Nietzsche into their own writings, speeches, and policies. To what extent were they accurate and justified in doing so?

In my judgment on this complicated question, a split decision is called for. In several very important respects, the Nazis were perfectly justified in seeing Nietzsche as a forerunner and as an intellectual ally. And in several important respects, Nietzsche would properly have been horrified at the misuse of his philosophy by the Nazis.

Let us start with the key differences between Nietzsche and the Nazis. Here I want to focus on five important points.

28. On the "blond beast" and racism

Take the phrase "the blond beast."

In recoiling from what he saw as a flaccid nineteenth-century European culture, Nietzsche often called longingly for "some pack of blond beasts of prey, a conqueror and master race which, organized for war and with the ability to organize, unhesitatingly lays its terrible claws upon a populace."[87] And he spoke of

> "[t]he deep and icy mistrust the German still arouses today whenever he gets into a position of power is an echo of that inextinguishable horror with which Europe observed for centuries that raging of the Blond Germanic beast."

And again inspirationally about what one finds

> "at the bottom of all these noble races the beast of prey, the splendid blond beast, prowling about avidly in search of spoil and victory; this hidden core needs to erupt from time to time, the animal has to get out again and go back to the wilderness."[88]

What are we to make of these regular positive mentions of the "blond beast"? It is clear what the Nazis made of them—an endorsement by Nietzsche of the racial superiority of the German Aryan type.

But for those who have read the original Nietzsche, that interpretation clearly takes Nietzsche's words out of context. In context, the "blond beast" that Nietzsche refers to is the lion, the great feline predator with the shaggy blond mane and the terrific roar. Nietzsche does believe that the Germans once, a long time ago, manifested the spirit of the lion—but they were not unique in that regard. The spirit and power of the lion have been manifested by peoples of many races.

To see this, let us put one of the quotations in full con-

---

[87] GM 2:17.
[88] GM 1:11.

text. The quotation begins this way: "at the bottom of all these noble races the beast of prey, the splendid blond beast, prowling about avidly in search of spoil and victory; this hidden core needs to erupt from time to time, the animal has to get out again and go back to the wilderness …"

Now let us complete the sentence as Nietzsche wrote it: "the Roman, Arabian, Germanic, Japanese nobility, the Homeric heroes, the Scandinavian Vikings—they all shared this need."[89]

So Nietzsche clearly is using the lion analogically and comparing its predatory power to the predatory power that humans of many different racial types have manifested. Nietzsche here lists six different racial and ethnic groups, and the Germans are not special in that list. So while Nietzsche does endorse a strongly biological basis for cultures, he does not endorse racism of the sort that says any one race is biologically necessarily superior to any other.

This is a clear difference with the Nazis. The Nazis were racist and thought of the Germanic racial type as superior to all others the world over. Nietzsche disagreed.

This leads us directly to a second major point of difference.

29. On contemporary Germans: the world's hope or contemptible?

While the Nazis put the German-Aryan racial type first, Nietzsche is almost never complimentary about his fellow Germans. In Nietzsche's view, Germany has slipped into flabbiness and whininess. Germany once was something to be awed and feared, but Germany in the nineteenth century has become a nation of religious revivalism, socialism, and movements towards democracy and equality.

Whatever special endowments the Germans once possessed they have lost. Nietzsche makes this clear when speak-

---

[89] *GM* 1:11.

ing about the Germany of the nineteenth-century: "between the old Germanic tribes and us Germans there exists hardly a conceptual relationship, let alone one of blood."[90] So rather than being proud of their ancient history and accomplishments, Nietzsche believes Germans of his day should feel ashamed by comparison.

At the same time, German intellectual and cultural life is prominent the world over—and Nietzsche deplores that fact. Contemporary Germany is a center of softness and slow decay, so Nietzsche believes that Germany's weaknesses are infecting the rest of the world. As he puts it in *The Will to Power*, "Aryan influence has corrupted all the world."[91]

So rather than celebrating contemporary Germany and its power, as the Nazis would do, Nietzsche is disgusted by contemporary Germany.

This leads us to a third major point of difference.

30. On anti-Semitism: valid or disgusting?

The most repulsive sign of Germany's decline, Nietzsche writes—and this may be initially surprising—is its hatred of the Jews, its virulent and almost-irrational anti-Semitism.

Nietzsche, we know, has said some harsh things about the Jews—but again, that is a set of issues that is easily misinterpreted, so we must be careful.

In connection with all of the negative things Nietzsche has said about the Jews, we must also note the following.

Nietzsche speaks of "the anti-Jewish stupidity" of the Germans.[92] He speaks of those psychologically disturbed indi-

---

[90] *GM* 1:11.
[91] *WP* 142; 145.
[92] *BGE* 251.

viduals who are most consumed with self-hatred and envy. He uses the French word *ressentiment* to describe such nauseating individuals and says that such *ressentiment* is "studied most easily in anarchists and anti-Semites."[93]

Pathological dishonesty is a symptom of such repulsive characters: "An antisemite certainly is not any more decent because he lies as a matter of principle."[94]

So, to summarize: Nietzsche saves some of his most condemnatory language for Germans who hate Jews—he considers them to be liars, stupid, disturbed, self-hating pathological cases for psychologists with strong stomachs to study.

So it seems a reasonable inference that Nietzsche would have been disgusted by the Nazis, for the Nazis absorbed into their ideology the worst possible kind of anti-Semitism and pursued their anti-Jew policies almost to the point of self-destruction.[95]

31. On the Jews: admirable or despicable?

But how does this fit with the harsh things we know Nietzsche said about the Jews? This takes us to a fourth point of difference between Nietzsche and the Nazis.

For all of the negative things Nietzsche says about the Jews, he also respects them and gives them high praise.

Here is a representative quotation from *Beyond Good and Evil*: "The Jews, however, are beyond any doubt the strongest, toughest, and purest race now living in Europe."[96]

---

[93] *GM* 2:11.
[94] *A* 55.
[95] Connecting here to the fascinating "What-if" history question: What if the Nazis had put the Holocaust on hold and devoted the vast resources used there instead to military purposes where needed in WWII?
[96] *BGE* 251.

Here is another, from *The Antichrist*: "Psychologically considered, the Jewish people are a people endowed with the toughest vital energy, who, placed in impossible circumstances . . . divined a power in these instincts with which one could prevail against 'the world.'"[97]

He again praises the Jews for having the strength to rule Europe if they chose to: "That the Jews, if they wanted it—or if they were forced into it, which seems to be what the anti-Semites want—could even now have preponderance, indeed quite literally mastery over Europe, that is certain; that they are not working and planning for that is equally certain."[98]

And in another book, Nietzsche compares the Jews favorably to the Germans—in fact, he identifies a way in which the Jews are superior to the Germans: "Europe owes the Jews no small thanks for making its people more logical, for cleaner intellectual habits—none more so than the Germans, as a lamentably *deraisonnable* race that even today first needs to be given a good mental drubbing."[99]

But how can all this praise of the Jews fit with the rest of what he says about the Jews?

One important distinction here is between blaming the Jews of several millennia ago for devising the slave morality and foisting it upon the world—and between evaluating the Jews of today as inheritors of a cultural tradition that has enabled them to survive and even flourish despite great adversity. In the former case, Nietzsche assigns blame to the Jews and condemns them for subverting human greatness—but in the second case he would at the very least have to grant, however grudgingly, that the Jews have hit upon a survival strategy and kept their cultural identity for well over two thousand years. How many other cultures can make that claim? The list is extremely short. And for that the Jews deserve praise.

---

[97] *A* 24.
[98] *BGE* 251.
[99] *GS* 348.

32. On Judaism and Christianity: opposite or identical?

One more key difference between Nietzsche and the Nazis is important, and that is their views on Christianity. Nietzsche consistently states that Judaism and Christianity are allies, both stemming from the same source, both advocating a religious ethic that puts the weak, the sick, and the humble first. As with Judaism, Christian morality is a slave morality.

Christianity, he writes, is "a rebellion of everything that crawls on the ground against that which has height."[100]

The Christians, he writes, "did not know how to love their god except by crucifying man."[101] And for that great crime against humanity, Nietzsche says: "I condemn Christianity. I raise against the Christian church the most terrible of all accusations that any accuser ever uttered. It is to me the highest of all conceivable corruptions."[102]

So Christianity does not escape Nietzsche's wrath, just as the slave morality of the Jews did not escape his wrath—and for the same reason: Christianity is an extension and purification of moral themes first developed within Judaism. In Nietzsche's own words: "In Christianity, all of Judaism . . . attains its ultimate mastery as the art of lying in a holy manner. The Christian, the *ultima ratio* of the lie, is the Jew once more—even three times more."[103]

This identification of Christianity with Judaism also separates Nietzsche from the Nazis, for the Nazis took great pains to distinguish the Jews and the Christians, condemning Judaism and embracing a generic type of Christianity.

Early in the Nazi Party's history, in its founding document, the 1920 Program, point 24 states the following: "The party, as such, stands for positive Christianity, without, how-

---

[100] *A* 43.
[101] *Z* 2: "On Priests."
[102] *A* 62.
[103] *A* 44.

ever, allying itself to any particular denomination. It combats the Jewish-materialistic spirit."

The use of Christian themes and imagery was prominent in Nazi propaganda throughout the 1920s.

In Joseph Goebbels's semi-autobiographical novel, the main character Michael is portrayed as a hybrid Christ-figure and German martyr. And in a 1935 interview, Goebbels was so concerned to separate Christianity from Judaism that he went as far as to deny that Jesus was a Jew.

Adolf Hitler argued that the Christians and Jews were fundamentally opposed religions[104] and himself sounded Christian moral themes explicitly in public pronouncements such as this one:

> When I came to Berlin a few weeks ago ...
> the luxury, the perversion, the iniquity, the
> wanton display, and the Jewish materialism
> disgusted me so thoroughly, that I was almost
> beside myself. I nearly imagined myself to be
> Jesus Christ when He came to His Father's
> temple and found it taken by the money-
> changers. I can well imagine how He felt when
> He seized a whip and scourged them out.[105]

---

[104] Hitler 1925, 307.

[105] Hitler, quoted in Langer, http://www.ess.uwe.ac.uk/documents/osssection1.htm (viewed July 25, 2006). Hitler also claimed: "By warding off the Jews, I struggle for the work of the Lord" (quoted in Lilla 1997, p. 38).

33. Summary of the five differences

We have five significant partings of the ways between Nietzsche and the Nazis:

1. The Nazis believe the German Aryan to be racially superior—while Nietzsche believes that the superior types can be manifested in any racial type.

2. The Nazis believe contemporary German culture to be the highest and the best hope for the world—while Nietzsche holds contemporary German culture to be degenerate and to be infecting the rest of the world.

3. The Nazis are enthusiastically anti-Semitic—while Nietzsche sees anti-Semitism to be a moral sickness.

4. The Nazis hate all things Jewish—while Nietzsche praises the Jews for their toughness, their intelligence, and their sheer survival ability.

5. And finally, the Nazis see Christianity to be radically different and much superior to Judaism—while Nietzsche believes Judaism and Christianity to be essentially the same, with Christianity being in fact a worse and more dangerous variation of Judaism.

Those five points identify important differences and lend support to those interpreters of Nietzsche who complain about simplistic identifications of Nietzsche as a proto-Nazi philosopher.[106]

But there are equally important ways in which the Nazis were right on target in seeing Nietzsche as an intellectual ally.

---

[106] E.g., Walter Kaufmann 1954, p. 14.

Part 7. Nietzsche as a Proto-Nazi

34. Anti-individualism and collectivism

We know that the National Socialists were thoroughly collectivistic and strongly anti-individualistic. For them the relevant groups were the Germanic Aryans—and all the others. Individuals were defined by their group identity, and individuals were seen only as vehicles through which the groups achieved their interests. The Nazis rejected the Western liberal idea that individuals are ends in themselves: to the Nazis individuals were merely servants of the groups to which they belong.

The anti-individualism of the Nazis was most blatant in their treatment of Jews. They did not see Jews as individuals with moral significance and rights—rather they saw members of a group they wished to destroy. This meant, as a matter of policy, that the Nazis were uncaring about the lives of individuals and were willing to kill as many individuals as was necessary to achieve their group's advantage.

Even within their own group, the Nazis did not see Aryan/Germans fundamentally as individuals. They saw them as members of the *Volk*, the German people, the group to which they owed service, obedience, and even their lives.

Nietzsche has a reputation for being an individualist. There certainly are individualist elements in Nietzsche's philosophy, but in my judgment his reputation for individualism is often much overstated.

When we speak of philosophies as being individualist or collectivist, three key points are at issue.

First, we ask: Do individuals shape their own identities—or are their identities created by forces beyond their control? For example, do individuals have the capacity to decide their own beliefs and form their own characters—or are individuals molded and shaped primarily by their biological inheritances or culturally by the groups they are born into and raised by?

Second, we ask: Are individuals ends in themselves, with their own lives and purposes to pursue—or do individuals exist for the sake of something beyond themselves to which they are expected to subordinate their interests?

Third, we ask: Do the decisive events in human life and history occur because individuals, generally exceptional individuals, make them happen—or are the decisive events of history a matter of collective action or larger forces at work?

Let us take the first issue—whether individuals shape themselves significantly or whether they are the product of forces beyond their control. Only in an attenuated way does Nietzsche believe that individuals shape their own characters and destiny—to a great extent he is determinist, believing that individuals are a product of their biological heritage. As he puts it in *Beyond Good and Evil*, "One cannot erase from the soul of a human being what his ancestors liked most to do and did most constantly."[107] Any given individual's thoughts, feelings, and actions, are an expression of an underlying set of traits that the individual inherited. Whether one is a sheep or a wolf is a matter of biology—one does not choose or shape oneself significantly—so to that extent it makes no sense to hold individuals responsible for who they are and what they become.[108]

What about the second issue—does Nietzsche believe that individuals are ends in themselves, that they exist for their own sake? Emphatically not. Here I think many casual read-

---

[107] *BGE* 264.
[108] "There is only aristocracy of birth, only aristocracy of blood" (*WP* 942).

ings of Nietzsche get him dead wrong. Take an initial obvious point: Nietzsche has nothing but contempt for the vast majority of the population, believing them to be sheep and a disgrace to the dignity of the human species. Their individual lives have no value in themselves. This is Nietzsche's point in the following quotation, in which he denies explicitly that his philosophy is individualistic: "My philosophy aims at ordering of rank not at an individualistic morality."[109] Nietzsche believes that most individuals have no right to exist and—more brutally—he asserts that if they were sacrificed or slaughtered that would be an improvement. In Nietzsche's own words: "mankind in the mass sacrificed to the prosperity of a single stronger species of man—that would be an advance."[110] And again: "One must learn from war: one must learn to sacrifice many and to take one's cause seriously enough not to spare men."[111] It is hard to see as an individualist anyone who sees no value in the lives of the vast majority of individuals. And it is hard to see as an individualist someone who would sacrifice those individuals in the name of improving the species. *Improving the species* is a collectivist goal, and measuring the value of individuals in terms of their value to the species and sacrificing those who do not measure up—that is textbook collectivism.

This connects directly to the value Nietzsche sees in the few great individuals who crop up in each generation. It is his powerfully poetic rhetoric in speaking of those exceptional individuals that gives Nietzsche his reputation for individualism. But it is important to note that Nietzsche does not see even those exceptional individuals as ends in themselves—and he does not exempt them from the sacrifice either. The point of becoming exceptional is not to advance one's own life but to improve the human species—in fact to get beyond the human species to a higher species-type: the overman. As Nietzsche

---

[109] *WP* 287. Morality is a social product: it arises "when a greater individual or a collective-individual, for example the society, the state, subjugates all other single ones ... and orders them into a unit" (*HH* 1.99).
[110] *GM* II:12.
[111] *WP* 982.

says repeatedly, "Not 'mankind' but overman is the goal!"[112] Nietzsche's goal is a collectivist one—to bring about a new, future, higher species of man—overman. This is the significance of his exhortations about the *Übermensch,* the overman, the superman.

So it seems that for Nietzsche *none of us*, whether weak or strong, exist for our own sakes. In direct contrast to individualists who believe that individuals' lives are their own to find and create value within, Nietzsche's belief is that our lives have value only to the extent we fulfill a goal beyond our lives—the creation of a stronger species. And on that general collectivist end, Nietzsche has an important point in common with the Nazis.

There is also the third sub-issue of individualism—whether the decisive events in human life and history occur because individuals, generally exceptional individuals, make them happen, or whether individuals are pawns of greater historical forces. Here the Nazis' theory and practice were a combination of both. They believed in and utilized mass-movement politics, seeing their political movement as the vehicle through which a powerful cultural force—the German *Volk*—was asserting its historical destiny. At the same time, the Nazis held that those powerful historical forces singled out some special individuals to perform special tasks and that destiny spoke through those special individuals. This, at any rate, was Hitler's firm belief when he made statements such as the following: "I carry out the commands that Providence has laid upon me"; and "No power on earth can shake the German Reich now, Divine Providence has willed it that I carry through the fulfillment of the Germanic task."[113]

In invoking Divine Providence, Hitler is drawing upon a long philosophical tradition that goes back most famously to the German philosopher Georg Hegel, with his World-Historical Individuals—those individuals such as Julius Caesar

---

[112] *WP* 1001.

[113] Hitler, quoted in Langer, http://www.ess.uwe.ac.uk/documents/osssection1.htm.

and Napoleon Bonaparte, who, on Hegel's view, were vehicles through which the Spiritual forces of history operated. That tradition goes back even further in religious interpretations of history.

Think, for example, of religious prophets. Prophets are special individuals within a religious tradition. The prophet, though, is not special *as an individual*—he is not an individual who has acquired his powers through his own efforts and who has created his own new and unique vision. Rather the prophet is special *only* because God has chosen him and because God is speaking through him. The prophet is totally a tool of God—his power comes from God and he

The Prophet Isaiah,
Raffaello Sanzio

is a mouthpiece through which God speaks his message. He is a localized vehicle through which the real force—namely, God—works.

Now let us return to Nietzsche. Nietzsche is an atheist, yet he offers a secular version of the same theory.

Nietzsche's power force is not religious or spiritual force, but a biological one. His great men—prophets like the Zarathustras who may be among us and those who are to come—are special individuals in whom powerful evolutionary forces have converged to create something remarkable. And those powerful evolutionary forces are working through those Zarathustras to achieve something even more remarkable—the overman. Such exceptional individuals do not develop and use power; power develops and uses those individuals. Individuals are only the tools, the vehicles. This is what Nietzsche is getting at when he says that every "living creature values many things higher than life itself; yet out of this evaluation itself speaks—the will to power."[114]

Note what Nietzsche is saying the real causal power is: The *will to power* works *through* those individuals; it is *not* that those individuals develop and use power.

There is legitimate controversy among scholars over this interpretation of Nietzsche, but to the extent this interpretation is true it does undermine Nietzsche's reputation as an individualist and strengthens the claim the Nazis have on him as a philosophical forerunner.

35. Conflict of groups

A second major point of agreement between Nietzsche and the Nazis is their view of conflict. For both, conflict is the fundamental human reality. Both believe firmly that life is a matter of some individuals and groups gaining at the expense of others.

The Nazis were clear about this in theory and practice. They did not believe it possible for Aryans and Jews to live in harmony. Nor did the Nazis believe that Germany could live in harmony with the liberal capitalist nations of the West.

In the liberal capitalist nations, by contrast, many economists and politicians had come to believe that conflict and war may become a thing of the past. The productive power of the Industrial Revolution was creating great wealth and surpluses, and those surpluses were leading to increased trade between nations that was mutually beneficial. Trade was a powerful harmonizing force, leading nations to want to do business with each other rather than make war.[115]

---

[114] Z 2:12.

[115] For example, the great British politician Richard Cobden argued that commerce is "the grand panacea, which, like a beneficent medical discovery, will serve to inoculate with the healthy and saving taste for civilization all the nations of the world" (Cobden 1903, p. 36). Consider also Norman Angell, speaking to the Institute of Bankers in London on January 17, 1912,

The Nazis rejected that view and argued that recent economic history was a matter of the Jews and the capitalists advancing their interests at the expense of Germany's.

Nietzsche shares wholly with the Nazis the general point about zero-sum conflict. In his words, "The well-being of the majority and the well-being of the few are opposite viewpoints of value."[116] But even more strongly, he believes that this conflict is not merely a matter of historical and cultural accident but is built into the requirements of life:

> Here one must think profoundly to the very basis and resist all sentimental weakness: life itself is *essentially* appropriation, injury, conquest of the strange and weak, suppression, severity, obtrusion of peculiar forms, incorporation and at the least, putting it mildest, exploitation.[117]

The horse eats the grass; the lion kills the horse; the man rides the horse and kills the lion. Life is an ongoing struggle between strong and weak, predator and prey. Cooperation and trade are possible, but they are superficial interludes between more fundamental animal facts about life. As Nietzsche again puts it: "'Life always lives at the expense of other life'—he who does not grasp this has not taken even the first

---

on "The Influence of Banking on International Relations": "commercial interdependence, which is the special mark of banking as it is the mark of no other profession or trade in quite the same degree — the fact that the interest and solvency of one is bound up with the interest and solvency of many; that there must be confidence in the due fulfillment of mutual obligation, or whole sections of the edifice crumble, is surely doing a great deal to dem-onstrate that morality after all is not founded upon self-sacrifice, but upon enlightened self-interest, a clearer and more complete understanding of all the ties that bind us the one to the other. And such clearer understanding is bound to improve, not merely the relationship of one group to another, but the relationship of all men to all other men, to create a consciousness which must make for more efficient human co-operation, a better human society" (quoted in Keegan 1999, pp. 11-12).

[116] *GM*, end of First Essay note.
[117] *BGE* 259.

step toward honesty with himself."[118]

On this key point, Nietzsche and the Nazis agree.

Given that conflict is inescapable, the next question is: How will the conflicts be resolved?

36. Instinct, passion, and anti-reason

Hitler was fond of saying, in private, "What luck that men do not think."

Another significant point of agreement exists between Nietzsche and the Nazis: both agree that the great conflicts will not be solved rationally, through the processes of discussion, argument, persuasion, or diplomacy. Both Nietzsche and the Nazis are irrationalists in their view of human psychology—and this has important social and political implications.

Think about democracy for a moment. In particular, think about how much confidence in the power of reason that democracy requires. Democracy is a matter of decentralizing political power to individuals by, for example, giving each individual a vote. The assumption of democracy is that individuals have the ability to weigh and judge important matters and cast a responsible vote. The expectation is that members of democracies will have ongoing discussions and arguments about all sorts of issues, and that they will be able to assess the evidence, the arguments and counter-arguments. And they will be able to learn from their mistakes and, when appropriate, change their votes the next time around.

It is not an accident that neither Nietzsche nor the Nazis were advocates of either democracy or reason.

Hitler considered a highly-developed intellect to be a weakness and too much reliance on reason to be a sickness. Germany's recent problems, he believed, stemmed from too much thinking. "The intellect has grown autocratic, and has become a disease of life." What Germany required was *passion*,

---

[118] *WP* 369.

a storm of emotion arising from deeply rooted instincts and drives: "Only a storm of glowing passion can turn the destinies of nations, but this passion can only be roused by a man who carries it within himself." [119] Consequently, German training and propaganda were not directed toward presenting facts and arguments but rather to arousing the passions of the masses. Reason, logic, and objectivity were beside the point. "We are not objective, we are German," said Hans Schemm, the first Nazi Minister of Culture.[120]

Here again there is an important connection to Nietzsche. Nietzsche too sees an opposition between conscious reason and unconscious instinct, and he disparages those who stress rationality—those who engage in what he calls the "ridiculous overestimation and misunderstanding of consciousness."[121] In his own words, it is "'Rationality' against instinct,"[122] and he believes that rationality is the *least* useful guiding power humans possess. Humans came out of a long evolutionary line that relied on drives and instincts—and those drives and instincts served us well for millennia. Yet men eventually became settled, tamed, and civilized, and they lost something crucial:

> [I]n this new world they no longer possessed their former guides, their regulating, unconscious and infallible drives: they were reduced to thinking, inferring, reckoning, co-ordinating cause and effect, these unfortunate creatures; they were reduced to their 'consciousness,' their weakest and most fallible organ![123]

Note that Nietzsche says our unconscious drives are *infallible*, if only we can find them within ourselves again. It

---

[119] Hitler, quoted in Langer, http://www.ess.uwe.ac.uk/documents/osssection1.htm.
[120] Schemm, quoted in Mosse 1966 xxxi.
[121] *GS* 11.
[122] *EH*: "The Birth of Tragedy" 1.
[123] *GM* II:16.

is our strongest, most assertive unconscious instinct that we should let rule our lives: "'instinct' is of all the kinds of intelligence that have been discovered so far—the most intelligent."[124]

And on this score, Nietzsche and the Nazis are in agreement: Both are fundamentally irrationalists—they do not think much of the power of reason, and they urge themselves and others to let their strongest passions and instincts well up within them and be released upon the world.

37. Conquest and war

Now put the above three points together: collectivism, conflict, and irrationalism. What will the social results be?

"Smash the Enemies of Greater Germany!"

If you believe wholeheartedly and passionately that your identity is found by merging yourself with your group—*and* that your group is locked in a mortal, zero-sum conflict with other groups—*and* that reason is superficial and that passion and instinct drive the world—then how will you assert yourself in that conflict?

For much of the nineteenth century, Western liberal capitalists had begun to wonder, hopefully, whether war was a thing of the past. In their judgment, progress had been made: During the Enlightenment of the eighteenth century, much of the West had embraced the idea of individual rights—the idea that each individual has rights to life, liberty, property, the pursuit of happiness. In the nineteenth century, those rights had been extended in practice to women and slavery had been eliminated. Also in the nineteenth century came the full real-

---

[124] *BGE* 218.

ization of the power of the Industrial Revolution and the idea that through technology and capitalism, economic production could be increased dramatically.

As a result, the liberal capitalists of the nineteenth century came to believe that we could solve the problem of poverty and eliminate most of our conflicts over wealth. They believed that with rising wealth and education, rational people could learn to respect each others' rights, that there was more to be gained from trade than from war, and that peace was a natural state that mankind could achieve. The horrors of war could become a thing of the past.[125]

We know from tragic twentieth-century history the National Socialists' eagerness to use war as their primary tool for achieving their international goals. We know their praising as fundamental the martial spirit and the beauty of the warrior soul. We know of their total recasting of education of children to achieve, as Hitler wanted "a brutal, domineering, fearless, cruel youth. Youth must be all that. It must bear pain. There must be nothing weak and gentle about it. The free, splendid beast of prey must once again flash from its eyes."[126]

---

[125] Richard Cobden in 1835: "The middle and industrious classes of England can have no interest apart from the preservation of peace. The honours, the fame, the emoluments of war belong not to them; the battle-plain is the harvest-field of the aristocracy, watered with the blood of the people." Also John Stuart Mill: "It is commerce which is rapidly rendering war obsolete, by strengthening and multiplying the personal interests which are in natural opposition to it" (1909). Again Mill: "Finally, commerce first taught nations to see with good will the wealth and prosperity of one another. Before, the patriot, unless sufficiently advanced in culture to feel the world his country, wished all countries weak, poor, and ill-governed, but his own: he now sees in their wealth and progress a direct source of wealth and progress to his own country. It is commerce which is rapidly rendering war obsolete, by strengthening and multiplying the personal interests which are in natural opposition to it. And it may be said without exaggeration that the great extent and rapid increase of international trade, in being the principal guarantee of the peace of the world, is the great permanent security for the uninterrupted progress of the ideas, the institutions, and the character of the human race" (1909, Book III, Chapter XVII, Section 14).
[126] Hitler, 1933.

The "beast of prey" phrase is again rhetoric inspired directly by Nietzsche. On the importance and nobility of war, Nietzsche and the Nazis were in almost full agreement. Nietzsche praised war and urged its coming. He wished for a great purge that would wipe out most humans whose lives he thought worthless and an embarrassment to the human species. "All-too-many live, and all-too-long they hang on their branches. Would that a storm came to shake all this worm-eaten rot from the tree!"[127]

But he also longed for war as a means to inspire those humans who have potential to advance us toward the overman. To that end, Nietzsche believed that war is absolutely indispensable:

> *War essential.* It is vain rhapsodizing and sentimentality to continue to expect much (even more, to expect a very great deal) from mankind, once it has learned not to wage war. For the time being, we know of no other means to imbue exhausted peoples, as strongly and surely as every great war does, with that raw energy of the battleground, that deep impersonal hatred, that murderous coldbloodedness with a good conscience, that communal, organized ardor in destroying the enemy, that proud indifference to great losses, to one's own existence and to that of one's friends, that muted, earthquake-like convulsion of the soul.[128]

And against those who believe that we have entered a more peaceful era and that perhaps war is no longer necessary, Nietzsche reminds us, in an especially chilling quotation: "The beginnings of everything great on earth [are] soaked in blood thoroughly and for a long time."[129]

---

[127] *Z*, First Part, "On Free Death."
[128] *HAH* 477.
[129] *GM* II, 6.

On this score, the Nazis were thoroughly Nietzschean. Rather than pushing for a recognition of the mutuality of human interests, as Western liberal capitalists had been doing for much of the nineteenth century—and rather than seeking reasonable and peaceful diplomatic solutions to the normal collisions of international politics—the Nazis committed fundamentally to war as their primary means of self-regeneration and dominance over the rest of the world.

38. Authoritarianism

A fifth and final set of themes link Nietzsche with the Nazis. Both were anti-democratic, anti-capitalistic, and anti-liberal.

Dem Führer die Treue

"Be true to the Führer"

The Nazis were not friends of democracy, but they were extremely effective players of democracy. They announced from the beginning, in their 1920 founding Party Program, their authoritarian principles. Nonetheless, finding themselves in the democratic system that was the Weimar Republic, they played mostly by the rules and out-democracied the other political parties. They used democracy to achieve anti-democratic ends.

Nietzsche's political views are less developed and more ambiguous, but it is clear he favors some sort of aristocracy. "What is serious for me," Nietzsche wrote in *Beyond Good and Evil*, is "the 'European problem' as I understand it, the cultivation of a new caste that will rule Europe."[130] Again, while Nietzsche is unspecific, he does not necessarily mean an official political aristocracy—he more likely means the *de facto* rule by an exceptional few, whatever the formal and official political

---

[130] *BGE* 251.

structures are. In this way, even though Nietzsche despises the impulses that give rise to democracy, he does not worry much about the actual political dominance of democratic forms of government. Those forms of government, he believes, will simply become instruments through which the exceptional individuals, most likely from behind the scenes, will achieve their goals. As Nietzsche puts it, democracy will be a tool of "a master race, the future 'masters of the earth' … philosophical men of power and artist-tyrants" who will "employ democratic Europe as their most pliant and supple instrument for getting hold of the destinies of the earth."[131]

Nietzsche is not programmatic about what form the new aristocratic class will take or what specific goals it will pursue. He believes that will be up to the overmen themselves—they will create their own values and shape the vehicles of their realization. And Nietzsche did not think of himself as an overman—merely as a herald of their coming. But Nietzsche is extremely clear that any social method, however brutal, will be legitimate should the new aristocrats desire it. A healthy aristocracy, he puts it forcefully, "accepts with a good conscience the sacrifice of untold human beings, who, for its sake, must be reduced and lowered to incomplete human beings, to slaves, to instruments."[132]

That is certainly anti-liberal and fits well with Nietzsche's self-assessment that he is "not by any means 'liberal'."[133]

In addition to dismissing liberalism, Nietzsche dismisses capitalism as a dehumanizing economic system[134] and rejects individualism when it comes to matters of marriage and procreation. Marriage, he thought, should not be based on "idio-

---

[131] Note for *BGE*, quoted in Hunt 1991, p. 39.
[132] *BGE* 258.
[133] *GS* 377.
[134] *D* 2 6.

syncrasy"—that is, upon love and personal sexual attraction.[135] Rather, he suggested, marriage should be state-organized for breeding purposes.[136]

On all those points, the Nazis can and did find inspiration in Nietzsche.

39. Summary of the five similarities

Again to summarize: we have five significant connections between Nietzsche and the Nazis:

1. The Nazis were strongly collectivistic, and Nietzsche, with some qualifications, also advances strongly collectivistic and anti-individualistic themes.

2. Both Nietzsche and the Nazis see zero-sum conflict as inescapable and as fundamental to the human condition.

3. Both are irrationalists in their psychological theories, downplaying radically the role that reason plays in life and emphasizing the power and the glory of instincts and feelings.

4. Both Nietzsche and the Nazis accept willingly—even longingly—that war is necessary, healthy, and even majestic.

5. And finally, both Nietzsche and the Nazis are anti-democratic, anti-capitalistic, and anti-liberal—and so, come the 1930s, the Nazis were in fundamental opposition to those nations to the West that were still broadly committed to democracy, capitalism, and liberalism.

---

[135] *TI* 9:39.
[136] *BGE* 251.

Part 8. Conclusion: Nazi and Anti-Nazi Philosophies

40. Hindsight and future resolve

We know from historical hindsight that it took a world war to defeat the Nazis. Tens of millions of human beings died in that war. Actual human beings who lived, loved, cried, had dreams—and then were killed. Millions of others had their lives damaged and disrupted seriously. Over and above all that, the economic and cultural costs—the wrecking of people's homes and possessions, the destruction of works of art, the obliteration of historical artifacts, and so on—those costs are incalculable.

The Nazis lost that war, but it was a close call, and there is no guarantee that it will not happen again.

And this is why it is important that we understand what really motivated National Socialism. By the 1930s, the Nazis had the entire political and economic muscle of Germany at their disposal—but more important than that, they had intellectual muscle behind them and they had a set of philosophical ideals that motivated and energized millions of people. That intellectual and idealistic power more than anything made the Nazis an awesome force to be reckoned with.

History has taught us that the philosophy and ideals the Nazis stood for were and are false and terribly destructive, but we do not do ourselves any favors by writing the Nazis off as madmen or as an historical oddity that will never happen again. The Nazis stood for philosophical and political principles that appealed to millions—that attracted some of the best minds of their generation—and that still command the minds and hearts of people in all parts of the world.

And that means we must face the National Socialists' philosophical and political ideals for what they actually are—we must understand them, know where they came from, and what intellectual and emotional power they have. Then and only then are we in a position to defeat them. We will be able to defeat them because we will understand their power and we will have more powerful arguments with which to fight back.

Arguing over philosophical and political ideals is often unpleasant. And the issues involved are often abstract, complicated, and emotionally difficult. But there are no shortcuts. Perhaps the best motivation for doing the hard work comes from reminding ourselves regularly and often how much *more* it costs to settle disputes by war.

We may not like that the Nazis had arguments and positions that many people find attractive. We might find it repulsive to take their arguments seriously. We might find it difficult to get inside their heads to see where they are coming from.

But we have a choice: We either fight those ideas in *theory* or we fight them in *practice*. We either fight them in the intellectual realm or we fight them on the battlefield. It might still come to fighting them on the battlefield—but that is always the most terrible option, the most expensive in every possible way, and the one we should avoid if there is any other way to defeat them.

So that means that defeating National Socialism *intellectually* is the strategy we should follow first. Defeating them intellectually means taking their positions seriously, understanding them, and knowing how to argue against them.

The second rule of politics is: *Know your enemy*. The first rule of politics is: *Know yourself*. Know what you stand for and why. Know what matters to you fundamentally and what you are willing to do to achieve it—and, when necessary, to fight to defend it.

That is a very large project, and that is why a culture's philosophers and other intellectuals do important work—or, if they get it wrong, great damage.

As a beginning to that project, let me indicate a clear direction to start in.

41. Principled anti-Nazism

Philosophically and politically, the Nazis stood for five major principles: They stood for collectivism, for instinct and passion, for war and conflict, for authoritarianism, and for socialism.

National Socialist Principles:

- Collectivism
- Instinct, passion, "blood"
- War and zero-sum conflict
- Authoritarianism
- Socialism

That means we can identify the principles that, in each case, are the direct opposite of what the Nazis stood for:

National Socialist Principles:	*Anti-Nazi Principles:*
• Collectivism	• Individualism
• Instinct, passion, "blood"	• Reason
• War and zero-sum conflict	• Production and win/win trade
• Authoritarianism	• Liberalism
• Socialism	• Capitalism

- The Nazis stood for collectivism. The opposite of that is a philosophy of *individualism* that recognizes each individual's right to live for his or her own sake.

- The Nazis stood for instinct and passion as one's basic guides in life. The opposite of that is a philosophy of *reason* that has a healthy confidence in the power of evidence, logic, and judgment to guide one's life.

- The Nazis stood for war and conflict as the best way to achieve one's goals. The opposite of that is a philosophy that encourages *productiveness and trade* and the best way to achieve one's goals in life.

- The Nazis stood for political authoritarianism and top-down leadership. The opposite of that is a philosophy that leaves individuals maximum *freedom* to live their lives by their own choice and direction, respecting the equal right of other individuals to do the same.

- The Nazis stood for socialism and the principle of central direction of the economy for the common good. The opposite of that is the system of *free market capitalism*, with individual producers and consumers deciding for themselves what they will produce and what they will spend their money on.

As a start, the principles in the right-hand column are the best antidote to National Socialism we have going. Each of those principles is controversial in our time, and I expect they will continue to be so for generations to come. But they represent the starkest philosophical contrast to National Socialism possible, and they form the first line of defense against future incarnations of Nazism. There is no better place to start than understanding them thoroughly.

I will end on a provocative note: The Nazis knew what they stood for. Do we?

Part 9. Appendices

Appendix 1: NSDAP Party Program

Program of the National Socialist German Workers' Party

The Program of the German Workers' Party is a limited program. Its leaders have no intention, once its aims have been achieved, of establishing new ones, merely in order to insure the continued existence of the party by the artificial creations of discontent among the cases.

1. We demand, on the basis of the right of national self-determination, the union of all Germans in a Greater Germany.

2. We demand equality for the German nation among other nations, and the revocation of the peace treaties of Versailles and Saint-Germain.

3. We demand land (colonies) to feed our people and to settle our excess population.

4. Only a racial comrade can be a citizen. Only a person of German blood, irrespective of religious denomination, can be a racial comrade. No Jew, therefore, can be a racial comrade.

5. Noncitizens shall be able to live in Germany as guests only, and must be placed under alien legislation.

6. We therefore demand that every public office, no matter of what kind, and no matter whether it be national, state, or local office, be held by none but citizens.

    We oppose the corrupting parliamentary custom of making party considerations, and not character and ability, the criterion for appointments to official positions.

7. We demand that the state make it its primary duty to provide a livelihood for its citizens. If it should prove impossible to feed the entire population, the members of foreign nations (noncitizens) are to be expelled from Germany.

8. Any further immigration of non-Germans is to be prevented. We demand that all non-Germans who entered Germany after August 2, 1914, be forced to leave the Reich without delay.

9. All citizens are to possess equal rights and obligations.

10. It must be the first duty of every citizen to perform mental or physical work. Individual activity must not violate the general interest, but must be exercised within the framework of the community, and for the general good.

THEREFORE WE DEMAND

11. The abolition of all income unearned by work and trouble.

BREAK THE SLAVERY OF INTEREST

12. In view of the tremendous sacrifices of life and property imposed by any war on the nation, personal gain from the war must be characterized as a crime against the nation. We therefore demand the total confiscation of all war profits.

13. We demand the nationalization of all business enterprises that have been organized into corporations (trusts).

14. We demand profit-sharing in large industrial enterprises.

15. We demand the generous development of old age insurance.

16. We demand the creation and support of a healthy middle class, and the immediate socialization of the huge department stores and their lease, at low rates, to small tradesmen. We demand that as far as national, state, or municipal purchases are concerned, the utmost consideration be shown to small tradesmen.

17. We demand a land reform suitable to our national needs, and the creation of a law for the expropriation without compensation of land for communal purposes. We demand the abolition of ground rent, and the prohibition of all speculation in land.

18. We demand a ruthless battle against those who, by their activities, injure the general good. Common criminals, usurers, profiteers, etc., are to be punished by death, regardless of faith or race.

19. We demand that Roman law, which serves a materialist world order, be replaced by German law.

20. To open the doors of higher education—and thus to leading positions—to every able and hard-working German, the state must provide for a thorough restructuring of our entire educational system. The curricula of all educational institutions are to be brought into line with the requirements of practical life. As soon as the mind begins to develop, the schools must reach civic thought (citizenship classes). We demand the education, at state expense, of particularly talented children of poor parents, regardless of the latters' class or occupation.

21. The state must see to it that national health standards are raised. It must do so by protecting mothers and children, by prohibiting child labor, by promoting

physical strength through legislation providing for compulsory gymnastic by the greatest possible support for all organizations engaged in the physical training of youth.

22. We demand the abolition of the mercenary army and the creation of a people's army.

23. We demand legal warfare against intentional political lies and their dissemination through the press. To facilitate the creation of a German press, we demand:

(a) that all editors of, and contributors to, newspapers that appear in the German language be racial comrades;

(b) that no non-German newspaper may appear without the express permission of the government. Such papers may not be printed in the German language;

(c) that non-Germans shall be forbidden by law to hold any financial share in a German newspaper, or to influence it in any way.

We demand that the penalty for violating such a law shall be the closing of the newspapers involved, and the immediate expulsion of the non-Germans involved.

Newspapers which violate the general good are to be banned. We demand legal warfare against those tendencies in art and literature which exert an undermining influence on our national life, and the suppression of cultural events which violate this demand.

24. We demand freedom for all religious denominations, provided they do not endanger the existence of the state, or violate the moral and ethical feelings of the Germanic race.

The party, as such, stands for positive Christianity,

without, however, allying itself to any particular denomination. It combats the Jewish-materialistic spirit within and around us, and is convinced that a permanent recovery of our people can be achieved only from within, on the basis of

THE COMMON INTEREST BEFORE SELF-INTEREST

25. To implement all these points, we demand the creation of a strong central power in Germany. A central political parliament should possess unconditional authority over the entire Reich, and its organization in general.

Corporations based on estate and profession should be formed to apply the general legislation passed by that Reich in the various German states.

The leaders of the party promise to do everything that is in their power, and if need be, to risk their very lives, to translate this program into action.

Munich, February 24, 1920.

Appendix 2: Quotations on Nazi socialism and fascism

Socialism against individualism

"National socialism is the determination to create a new man. There will no longer exist any individual arbitrary will, nor realms in which the individual belongs to himself. The time of happiness as a private matter is over."

—Adolf Hitler[137]

"The concept of personal liberties of the individual as opposed to the authority of the state had to disappear; it is not to be reconciled with the principle of the nationalistic Reich. There are no personal liberties of the individual which fall outside of the realm of the state and which must be respected by the state. The member of the people, organically connected with the whole community, has replaced the isolated individual; he is included in the totality of the political people and is drawn into the collective action. There can no longer be any question of a private sphere, free of state influence, which is sacred and untouchable before the political unity. The constitution of the nationalistic Reich is therefore not based upon a system of inborn and inalienable rights of the individual."

—Ernst Rudolf Huber,[138] official spokesman for the National Socialist German Workers' Party, 1939

---

[137] Quoted in Joachim C. Fest, *Hitler*. New York: Harcourt Brace Jovanovich, 1974, p. 533.

[138] Huber, *Verfassungsrecht des grossdeutschen Reiches* (Hamburg, 1939), in Raymond E. Murphy, et al., ed., *National Socialism,* reprinted in *Readings on Fascism and National Socialism,* selected by Department of Philosophy, University of Colorado. Athens, OH: Swallow Press, 1952, p. 90.

"[O]ur German language has a word which in a magnificent way denotes conduct based on this spirit: doing one's duty [*Pflichterfüllung*]—which means serving the community instead of contenting oneself. We have a word for the basic disposition which underlies conduct of this kind in contrast to egoism and selfishness—idealism. By 'idealism' we mean only the ability of the individual to sacrifice himself for the whole, for his fellow men."

—Adolf Hitler,[139] 1925

"The State must act as the guardian of a millennial future in the face of which the wishes and the selfishness of the individual must appear as nothing and submit."

—Adolf Hitler[140]

"[S]ocialism is sacrificing the individual to the whole."

—Joseph Goebbels[141]

"THE COMMON INTEREST BEFORE SELF-INTEREST."

—NDSAP Program, Point 24, 1920

"We must rouse in our people the unanimous wish for power in this sense, together with the determination to sacrifice on the altar of patriotism, not only life and property, but also private views and preferences in the interests of the common welfare."

—Friedrich von Bernhardi,[142] 1912

---

[139] Hitler, "On Idealism and Winning the Masses Over," in Heinz Lubasz, ed., *Fascism: Three Major Regimes*. John Wiley & Sons: 1973, pp. 81-82.
[140] Hitler, *Mein Kampf*, translated by Ralph Manheim. Houghton Mifflin: 1971, p. 404.
[141] Goebbels, *Michael,* in Erich Fromm, *Escape from Freedom.* New York: Rinehart & Company, 1941, p. 233.
[142] Friedrich von Bernhardi. *Germany, the Next War,* translated by Allen H.

Socialist economics

"To put it quite clearly: we have an economic programme.
Point No. 13 in that programme demands the nationalisation
of all public companies, in other words socialisation, or what
is known here as socialism. ... the basic principle of my Party's
economic programme should be made perfectly clear and that
is the principle of authority ... the good of the community
takes priority over that of the individual. But the State should
retain control; every owner should feel himself to be an
agent of the State; it is his duty not to misuse his possessions
to the detriment of the State or the interests of his fellow
countrymen. That is the overriding point. The Third Reich
will always retain the right to control property owners. If you
say that the bourgeoisie is tearing its hair over the question
of private property, that does not affect me in the least. Does
the bourgeoisie expect some consideration from me? ...
The bourgeois press does me damage too and would like to
consign me and my movement to the devil. You are, after all
a representative of the bourgeoisie ... your press thinks it must
continuously distort my ideas. ... We do not intend to nail
every rich Jew to the telegraph poles on the Munich-Berlin
road."

— Adolf Hitler,[143] to R. Breiting, "bourgeois" newspaper
editor, 1931

"We are socialists, we are enemies of today's capitalistic
economic system for the exploitation of the economically
weak, with its unfair salaries, with its unseemly evaluation of

---

Powles. New York: E. Arnold, 1912, Chapter 5, p. 113.

[143] Hitler, in interview with Richard Breiting, 1931, published in Edouard
Calic, ed., "First Interview with Hitler," *Secret Conversations with Hitler: The
Two Newly-Discovered 1931 Interviews*. New York: John Day Co., 1971, pp.
31-35.

a human being according to wealth and property instead of responsibility and performance, and we are all determined to destroy this system under all conditions."

—Adolf Hitler,[144] 1927 speech

On "the money pigs of capitalist democracy": "Money has made slaves of us." "Money is the curse of mankind. It smothers the seed of everything great and good. Every penny is sticky with sweat and blood."

—Joseph Goebbels, [145] 1929

"The worker in a capitalist state—and that is his deepest misfortune—is no longer a living human being, a creator, a maker. He has become a machine. A number, a cog in the machine without sense or understanding. He is alienated from what he produces."

—Joseph Goebbels, [146] 1932 pamphlet

"'Private property' as conceived under the liberalistic economic order ... represented the right of the individual to manage and to speculate with inherited or acquired property as he pleased, without regard for the general interests ... German socialism had to overcome this 'private,' that is, unrestrained and irresponsible view of property. All property is common property. The owner is bound by the people and the Reich to the responsible management of his goods. His legal position is only justified when he satisfies this responsibility to the community."

—Ernst Rudolf Huber,[147] official Nazi Party spokesman, 1939

---

[144] Hitler, May 1, 1927; quoted in Toland 1976, p. 306.
[145] Goebbels, quoted in Orlow 1969, p. 87. And Goebbels 1929, in Mosse ed., 1966, p. 107.
[146] Goebbels 1932, "Those Damned Nazis" pamphlet.
[147] Huber, *Verfassungsrecht*, p. 91.

National Socialism, according to some later commentators

"Hitler was never a socialist."

—Ian Kershaw[148]

"Bastard movements like the National Socialism (Nazism) of twentieth-century Germany and Austria ..., save for the bare fact that they enforced central control of social policy, had nothing of socialism in them."

—Margaret Cole,[149] under "Socialism," in *The Encyclopedia of Philosophy*

"Stalinism is a pathology of socialism, Hitlerism being the apposite example for capitalism."

—Robert Heilbroner,[150] popular socialist author, 1980

"If there is one thing all Fascists and National Socialists agreed on, it was their hostility to capitalism."

—Eugen Weber,[151] historian of fascism

"[A]nti-Semitism was rife in almost all varieties of socialism."

—Sidney Hook,[152] socialist philosopher

---

[148] Kershaw, *Hitler: 1889-1936 Hubris*. New York: Norton, 1999, p. 448.

[149] Cole, "Socialism," *Encyclopedia of Philosophy*, ed. Paul Edwards. New York: Macmillan and Free Press, 1967. Vol. 7, pp. 467-70.

[150] Heilbroner, *Marxism: For and Against*. New York: Norton, 1980, p. 169.

[151] Weber, *Varieties of Fascism*. D. Van Nostrand, 1964, p. 47.

[152] Hook, "Home Truths About Marx," *Commentary* (September 1978), reprinted in *Marxism and Beyond*. Totowa, NJ: Rowman and Littlefield, 1983, p. 117.

"It is significant that the most important ancestors of National Socialism—Fichte, Rodbertus, and Lassalle—are at the same time acknowledged fathers of socialism."

—F. A. Hayek,[153] 1944

Socialism and authoritarianism

"The party is all-embracing. It rules our lives in all their breadth and depth. We must therefore develop branches of the party in which the whole of individual life will be reflected. Each activity and each need of the individual will thereby be regulated by the party as the representative of the general good. There will be no license, no free space, in which the individual belongs to himself. This is Socialism—not such trifles as the private possession of the means of production. Of what importance is that if I range men firmly within a discipline they cannot escape? Let them then own land or factories as much as they please. The decisive factor is that the State, through the party, is supreme over them, regardless whether they are owners or workers. All that, you see, is unessential. Our Socialism goes far deeper."

—Adolf Hitler[154]

"Our present political world-view, current in Germany, is based in general on the idea that creative, culture-creating force must indeed be attributed to the state."

—Adolf Hitler,[155] 1925

---

[153] Hayek, *The Road to Serfdom*. University of Chicago Press, 1944/1994, pp. 184-85.
[154] Hitler, quoted in Hermann Rauschning, *The Voice of Destruction*. New York: Putnam, 1940, p. 191.
[155] Hitler, *Mein Kampf*, p. 382.

"The first foundation for the creation of authority is always provided by popularity."

—Adolf Hitler[156]

"The advantage of ... an unwritten constitution over the formal constitution is that the basic principles do not become rigid but remain in a constant, living movement. Not dead institutions but living principles determine the nature of the new constitutional order."

—Ernst Rudolf Huber,[157] official spokesman for the National Socialist German Workers' (Nazi) Party, 1939

Against capitalism

"We German National Socialists have recognized that not international solidarity frees the peoples from the ties of international capital, but the *organized national force*. ...The National Socialist German Workers' Party asks you all to come ... to a GIANT DEMONSTRATION against the continued cheating of our people by the Jewish agents of the international world stock-exchange capital."

—Nazi Poster,[158] 1921

"It is not to save capitalism that we fight in Russia ... It is for a revolution of our own. ... If Europe were to become once more the Europe of bankers, of fat corrupt bourgeoisies ... *we should prefer Communism to win and destroy everything. We would rather have it all blow up than see this rottenness resplendent.* Europe

---

[156] Hitler, *Mein Kampf*, p. 518.
[157] Huber, *Verfassungsrecht*, p. 63.
[158] Nazi poster/handbill, in *Mein Kampf*. New York: Reynal & Hitchcock, 1941, Appendix, p. 541.

fights in Russia because it [i.e., Fascist Europe] is Socialist. ...
what interests us most in the war is the revolution to follow
... The war cannot end without the triumph of Socialist
revolution."

> —Léon Degrelle,[159] leading National Socialist figure,
> speaking on behalf of the Nazi SS in occupied Paris, 1943

"[W]e will do what we like with the bourgeoisie. ... We give
the orders; they do what they are told. Any resistance will be
broken ruthlessly."

> —Adolf Hitler,[160] 1931

"The internal and international criminal gang will either be
forced to work or simply exterminated."

> —Adolf Hitler,[161] 1931

"Today I will once more be a prophet. If the international
Jewish financiers, inside and outside Europe, succeed in
plunging the nations once more into a world war, then the
result will not be the Bolshevisation of the earth, and thus the
victory of Jewry, but the annihilation of the Jewish race in
Europe!"

> —Adolf Hitler,[162] 1939

---

[159] Degrelle, 1943. See Eugen Weber, *Varieties of Fascism*. D. Van Nostrand, 1964, p. 47. Degrelle was "a leading National Socialist figure, highly regarded by Hitler and by Himmler, speaking for the SS who would later publish and distribute the long speech, with the most revolutionary statements carefully italicized."

[160] Hitler, in Breiting, p. 36.

[161] Hitler, in Breiting, p. 86.

[162] Hitler, speaking in the Reichstag on January 30, 1939. http://www.bbc.co.uk/history/worldwars/genocide/hitler_speech_2.shtml

Historical roots: Jean-Jacques Rousseau

"Hitler is an outcome of Rousseau."
    —Bertrand Russell,[163] 1945

"Each member of the community gives himself to it at the instant of its constitution, just as he actually is, himself and all his forces, including all goods in his possession."
    —Jean-Jacques Rousseau[164]

"Whoever refuses to obey the general will will be forced to do so by the entire body; this means merely that he will be forced to be free."
    —Jean-Jacques Rousseau[165]

"The political body, therefore, is also a moral being which has a will; and this general will, which tends always to the conservation and well-being of the whole and of each part of it ... is, for all members of the state ... the rule of what is just or unjust."
    —Jean-Jacques Rousseau[166]

---

[163] Russell, *A History of Western Philosophy*. New York: Simon and Schuster, 1945, p. 685.
[164] Rousseau, *The Social Contract* (1762), translated by Donald Cress. Hackett, 1987. Book 1, Section 9.
[165] Rousseau, *The Social Contract*, Book 1, Section 7.
[166] Rousseau, *A Discourse on Political Economy*, in *Discourse on Political Economy; and, The Social Contract*, translated by Christopher Betts. Oxford University Press, 1994, p. 7.

"The State dominates the Nation because it alone represents it."

    —Adolf Hitler[167]

The state "ought to have a universal compulsory force to move and arrange each part in the manner best suited to the whole. Just as nature gives each man an absolute power over all his members, the social compact gives the body politic an absolute power over all its members." "We grant that each person alienates, by the social compact, only that portion of his power, his goods, and liberty whose use is of consequence to the community; but we must also grant that only the sovereign is the judge of what is of consequence."

    —Jean-Jacques Rousseau[168]

"For us the supreme law of the constitution is: whatever serves the vital interests of the nation is legal."

    —Adolf Hitler,[169] 1931

"A citizen should render to the state all the services he can as soon as the sovereign demands them."

    —Jean-Jacques Rousseau[170]

"I wish to give officials greater discretion. The State's authority will be increased thereby. I wish to transform the non-political criminal police into a political instrument of the highest State authority."

    —Adolf Hitler,[171] 1931

---

[167] Hitler, quoted in Albert Jay Nock, *Our Enemy the State* (1935). Reprinted by Libertarian Review Foundation (New York, 1989), p. 10.

[168] Rousseau, *The Social Contract*, Book 2, Section 4.

[169] Hitler, in Breiting, p. 86.

[170] Rousseau, *The Social Contract*, Book 2, Section 4.

[171] Hitler, in Breiting, p. 86.

Historical roots: Karl Marx

"[W]hen I was a worker I busied myself with socialist or, if you like, marxist [*sic*] literature."
    —Adolf Hitler,[172] 1931

"I have learned a great deal from Marxism, as I do not hesitate to admit. I don't mean their tiresome social doctrine or the materialist conception of history, or their absurd 'marginal utility' theories and so on. But I have learnt from their methods. The difference between them and myself is that I have really put into practice what these peddlers and pen-pushers have timidly begun. The whole of National Socialism is based on it. Look at the workers' sports clubs, the industrial cells, the mass demonstrations, the propaganda leaflets written specially for the comprehension of masses; all these new methods of political struggle are essentially Marxist in origin. All that I had to do was take over these methods and adapt them to our purpose. I had only to develop logically what Social Democracy repeatedly failed in because of its attempt to realize its evolution within the framework of democracy. National Socialism is what Marxism might have been if it could have broken its absurd and artificial ties with a democratic order."
    —Adolf Hitler[173]

"Besides, there is more that binds us to Bolshevism than separates us from it. There is, above all, genuine, revolutionary feeling, which is alive everywhere in Russia except where there are Jewish Marxists. I have always made allowance for this

---

[172] Hitler, in Breiting, p. 58.
[173] Hitler, quoted in Rauschning, p. 186.

circumstance, and given orders that former Communists are to be admitted to the party at once. The *petit bourgeois* Social-Democrat and the trade-union boss will never make a National Socialist, but the Communist always will."

—Adolf Hitler[174]

"What is the profane basis of Judaism? *Practical* need, *self-interest*. What is the worldly cult of the Jew? *Huckstering*. What is his worldly god? *Money*. Very well: then in emancipating itself from *huckstering* and *money*, and thus from real and practical Judaism, our age would emancipate itself. ... We discern in Judaism ... a universal *antisocial* element ...

"As soon as society succeeds in abolishing the *empirical* essence of Judaism—huckstering and its conditions—the Jew becomes *impossible* ... The social emancipation of the Jew is the *emancipation of society from Judaism*."

—Karl Marx,[175] "On the Jewish Question," 1843

"[I]t is quite enough that the scientific knowledge of the danger of Judaism is gradually deepened and that every individual on the basis of this knowledge begins to eliminate the Jew within himself, and I am very much afraid that this beautiful thought originates from none other than a Jew [i.e., Marx]."

—Adolf Hitler[176]

---

[174] Hitler, quoted in Rauschning, p. 131.
[175] Marx, "On the Jewish Question," in Robert Tucker, *The Marx-Engels Reader*. Second edition. New York: W. W. Norton & Co., 1978, pp. 48, 52.
[176] Hitler, quoted in Julius Carlebach, *Karl Marx and the Radical Critique of Judaism*. pp. 355-356; see also Praeger and Telushkin, *Why the Jews?* New York: Simon and Schuster, 1983, pp. 138-139.

"As I listened to Gottfried Feder's first lecture about the 'breaking of interest slavery,' I knew at once that this was a theoretical truth which would inevitably be of immense importance for the German people. ... The development of Germany was much too clear in my eyes for me not to know that the hardest battle would have to be fought, not against hostile nations, but against international capital.

"... Thus, it was the conclusions of Gottfried Feder that caused me to delve into the fundamentals of this field with which I had previously not been very familiar. I began to study again, and now for the first time really achieved an understanding of the content of ... Karl Marx's life effort. Only now did his *Kapital* become really intelligible to me ..."

—Adolf Hitler,[177] 1925

"Hitler admired Stalin, quite properly seeing himself as a mere infant in crime compared to his great exemplar."

—Doris Lessing[178]

"As National Socialists we see our program in our flag. In the *red* we see the social idea of the movement."

—Adolf Hitler, [179] *Mein Kampf*

"The Nazis were not conservatives. They were radicals, they were revolutionaries, and conservatives in Germany understood this."

—Thomas Childers,[180] American historian of World War II

---

[177] Hitler, *Mein Kampf*, pp. 213, 215.
[178] Lessing, *Walking in Shade*. Harper Collins, 1997, p. 262.
[179] Hitler, *Main Kampf*. New York: Reynal & Hitchcock, 1941, p. 737.
[180] Thomas Childers, "Lecture 5: The Nazi Breakthrough." *A History of Hitler's Empire*, 2nd ed., lecture series published by The Teaching Company, Chantilly, VA, 2001, minutes 5-6.

Comparing Italian Fascism and German National Socialism

"For Fascism, society is the end, individuals the means, and its whole life consists in using individuals as instruments for its social ends."

—Alfredo Rocco,[181] founder of Fascist theory, 1925

"Liberalism denied the State in the name of the individual; Fascism reasserts the rights of the State as expressing the real essence of the individual."

—Benito Mussolini[182]

"The State, in fact, as the universal ethical will, is the creator of right."

—Benito Mussolini,[183] 1932

"In Fascism the State is not a night-watchman, only occupied with the personal safety of the citizens."

—Benito Mussolini,[184] 1929

"As regards the Liberal doctrines, the attitude of Fascism is one of absolute opposition both in the political and in the economical field."

—Benito Mussolini,[185] 1932

---

[181] Rocco, "The Political Doctrine of Fascism" (address delivered at Perugia, August 30, 1925), reprinted in *Readings on Fascism and National Socialism*, selected by Dept. of Philosophy, University of Colorado. Athens, OH: Swallow Press, 1952, p. 35.

[182] In Charles F. Delzell, ed., *Mediterranean Fascism: 1919 - 1945*. New York: Harper & Row, 1970, p. 94.

[183] Mussolini, "The Doctrine of Fascism: Fundamental Ideas," *Enciclopedia Italiana*, 1932. Reprinted in Heinz Lubasz, ed., *Fascism: Three Major Regimes*. John Wiley & Sons: 1973, p. 41.

[184] Mussolini, "The Doctrine of Fascism," p. 21.

[185] Mussolini, "The Doctrine of Fascism," p. 18.

"Anti-individualistic, the Fascist conception of life stresses the importance of the State and accepts the individual only insofar as his interests as he coincides with those of the State ... . It is opposed to classical liberalism which arose as a reaction to absolutism and exhausted its historical function when the State became the expression of the conscience and will of the people. Liberalism denied the State in the name of the individual; Fascism reasserts the rights of the State as expressing the real essence of the individual ... Thus understood, Fascism is totalitarian, and the Fascist State—a synthesis and a unit inclusive of all values—interprets, develops, and potentiates the whole life of a people."

"The Fascist State, as a higher and more powerful expression of personality, is a force, but a spiritual one. It sums up all the manifestations of the moral and intellectual life of man. Its functions cannot therefore be limited to those of enforcing order and keeping the peace, as the liberal doctrine had it."

—Benito Mussolini,[186] 1932

"We do not, however, accept a bill of rights which tends to make the individual superior to the State and to empower him to act in opposition to society."

—Alfredo Rocco,[187] 1925

"All for the State; nothing outside the State; nothing against the State."

—Benito Mussolini[188]

---

[186] Mussolini, "The Doctrine of Fascism," pp. 93–94, 95.

[187] Rocco, "The Political Doctrine of Fascism" (address delivered at Perugia, August 30, 1925), reprinted in *Readings on Fascism and National Socialism*, p. 36.

[188] Mussolini, quoted in Ortega y Gasset, *The Revolt of the Masses*. New York: W. W. Norton & Company, 1993, p. 122.

Appendix 3: Quotations on German anti-Semitism

Martin Luther (1483-1546): "The Jews deserve to hang on gallows, seven times higher than ordinary thieves." And: "We ought to take revenge on the Jews and kill them."[189]

Immanuel Kant (1724-1804): The Jews are by nature "sharp dealers" who are "bound together by superstition." Their "immoral and vile" behavior in commerce shows that they "do not aspire to civic virtue," for "the spirit of usury holds sway amongst them." They are "a nation of swindlers" who benefit only "from deceiving their host's culture."[190]

Kant: "The euthanasia of Judaism is the pure moral religion."[191]

Johann Herder (1744-1803) quotes Kant from his lectures on practical philosophy: "*Every coward* is a liar; Jews, for example, not only in business, but also in common life."[192]

Johann Fichte (1762-1814): "A mighty state stretches across almost all the nations of Europe, hostile in intent and in constant strife with all others ... this is Jewry." Also: "As for giving them [the Jews] civil rights, I for one see no remedy but that their heads should be all cut off in one night and replaced with others in which there would not be one single Jewish idea."[193]

---

[189] Luther, quoted in Murphy 1999, p. 9.

[190] Kant, quoted in Weiss 1996, p. 67)

[191] Kant, *Streit der Fakultaten*, in *Werke* 11:321, quoted in Paul Lawrence Rose, *Revolutionary Antisemitism from Kant to Wagner* (Princeton, 1990), p. 96.

[192] Herder, quoted in Mack, 2003, p. 5.

[193] Fichte, quoted in Weiss 1996, pp. 72 and 68.

Ernst Moritz Arndt (1769-1860, professor at University of Bonn). Arndt was a poet, a historian, a deeply-religious Lutheran, and post-Kantian philosophical idealist whose hero was Arminius, who defeated the Romans in 9 C.E., thus saving the pure German soul from "contamination" by Latin races. According to Arndt, the Jews were "a rotten and degenerate race" that had "evil and worthless drives and desires."[194]

G. W. F. Hegel (1770-1831): Germany cannot assimilate the Jews because the Jews live an "animal existence that can only be secured at someone else's expense." Also: "Spirit alone recognizes spirit. They [the Jews] saw in Jesus only the man ... for He was only one like themselves, and they felt themselves to be nothing. The Jewish multitude was bound to wreck His attempt to give them the consciousness of something divine, for faith in something divine, something great, cannot make its home in a dunghill."[195]

Johann Fries (1773-1843, professor at University of Heidelberg): Fries was a Kantian logician, a disciple of Fichte, and influential among student nationalist societies. He called the Jews "rotten," "worthless cheats," "bloodsuckers," a "diseased people," argued they should be required to wear special signs indicating to others their race, and called for their "extermination."[196]

Karl Marx (1818-1883): "Let us consider the actual, worldly Jew—not the Sabbath Jew, as Bauer does, but the everyday Jew. Let us not look for the secret of the Jew in his religion, but

---

[194] Arndt, quoted in Weiss 1996, p. 74.
[195] Hegel. quoted in Weiss 1996, pp. 67 and 66.
[196] Fries, quoted in Weiss 1996, p. 74.

let us look for the secret of his religion in the real Jew. What is the secular basis of Judaism? Practical need, self-interest. What is the worldly religion of the Jew? Huckstering. What is his worldly God? Money. Very well then! Emancipation from huckstering and money, consequently from practical, real Jewry, would be the self-emancipation of our time .... We recognize in Jewry, therefore, a general present-time-oriented anti-social element, an element which through historical development—to which in this harmful respect the Jews have zealously contributed—has been brought to its present high level, at which it must necessarily dissolve itself. In the final analysis, the emancipation of the Jews is the emancipation of mankind from Jewry."[197]

Friedrich Nietzsche (1844-1900): "I have not met a German yet who was well disposed toward the Jews; and however unconditionally all the cautious and politically-minded repudiated real anti-Semitism, even this caution and policy are not directed against the species of this feeling itself but only against its dangerous immoderation."[198]

Adolf Hitler (1889-1945) in 1925: "I am convinced that I am acting as the agent of our Creator. By fighting off the Jews, I am doing the Lord's work." And in 1931: "The Jewish problem is a highly complex matter ... our ideology is opposed to the interests of the Chosen Race in that we abominate their dance around the Golden Calf. For racial and financial reasons the Jews are basically opposed to communism."[199]

---

[197] Marx, "On *The Jewish Question*," http://www.marxists.org/archive/marx/works/1844/jewish-question/. Viewed September 17, 2007.
[198] Nietzsche, *BGE* 251.
[199] Hitler, in interview with Richard Breiting, 1931, published in Edouard Calic, ed., "Second Interview with Hitler," *Secret Conversations with Hitler: The Two Newly-Discovered 1931 Interviews*. New York: John Day Co., 1971, p. 86.

Hitler: "Anti-Semitism is a useful revolutionary expedient."[200]

Sidney Hook (1902-1989), a socialist philosopher: "anti-Semitism was rife in almost all varieties of socialism."[201]

---

[200] Hitler, in Hermann Rauschning, *The Voice of Destruction: Hitler Speaks,* as quoted in George Seldes, *The Great Thoughts.* New York: Ballantine, p. 186.
[201] Hook, "Home Truths About Marx," *Commentary* (September 1978) reprinted in *Marxism and Beyond.* Totowa, NJ: Rowman and Littlefield, 1983, p. 117.

Appendix 4: Quotations on German militarism

Immanuel Kant (1724-1804): "War itself, if it is carried on with order and with a sacred respect for the rights of citizens, has something sublime in it, and makes the disposition of the people who carry it on thus only the more sublime, the more numerous are the dangers to which they are exposed and in respect of which they behave with courage. On the other hand, a long peace generally brings about a predominant commercial spirit and, along with it, low selfishness, cowardice, and effeminacy, and debases the disposition of the people."[202]

Kant: "Thus, at the stage of culture at which the human race still stands, war is an indispensable means for bringing it to a still higher stage."[203]

G. W. F. Hegel (1770-1831) on World-Historical Individuals, those whom the march of history has selected to advance its ends: "A World-historical individual is not so unwise as to indulge a variety of wishes to divide his regards. He is devoted to the One Aim, regardless of all else. It is even possible that such men may treat other great, even sacred interests, inconsiderately; conduct which is indeed obnoxious to moral reprehension. But so mighty a form must trample down many an innocent flower—crush to pieces many an object in its path."[204]

Leopold von Ranke (1795-1886), professor of history at Berlin and the most influential German historian of the nineteenth century. Ranke was deeply religious and a strong

---

[202] Kant, *Critique of Judgment* [1790]. Translated by J. H. Bernard (Haffner Press, 1951), § 28.
[203] Kant, "Speculative Beginning of Human History" [1786]. In *Perpetual Peace and Other Essays*, translated by Ted Humphrey (Hackett, 1983), 58/121.
[204] Hegel, *The Philosophy of History*. Translated by J. Sibree (Prometheus, 1991), p. 32.

believer in the divine mission of the German monarchical
state. "[P]ositive religion, which resists the vague flight into
liberalism, accords with my beliefs." "I know nothing since
the psalms where the idea of a religious monarchy has been
expressed more powerfully and more nobly. It has great
passages of historical truth." As historian A. J. P. Taylor put it,
speaking of Ranke and his followers, "they regarded the state,
whoever conducted it, as part of the divine order of things; and
they felt it their duty to acquiesce in that divine order. They
never opposed; they rarely protested."[205]

Heinrich Heine (1797-1856, German poet and essayist): "Not
only Alsace-Lorraine but all France and all Europe as well as
the whole world will belong to us."[206]

Max Stirner (1806-1856), a Young Hegelian philosopher.
While at university at Berlin, he was inspired by Hegel's
lectures and was a member of "The Free," a discussion group
that included Karl Marx, Friedrich Engels, and Ludwig
Feuerbach as members. "What does right matter to me? I have
no need of it ... . I have the right to do what I have the power
to do."[207]

Franz Felix Kuhn (1812-1881), philologist and folklorist:
"Must culture build its cathedrals upon hills of corpses, seas of

---

[205] Ranke, quoted in A. J. P. Taylor, "Ranke: The Dedicated Historian." *The Course of German History, A Survey of the Development of Germany since 1815* (Hamish Hamilton, 1945), p. 265.
[206] Heine, quoted in Darwin P. Kingsley, "Woodrow Wilson and the Doctrine of Sovereignty," *Addresses of the Empire Club of Canada*. Delivered October 17, 1918. Also posted at http://www.archive.org/stream/letushave-peaceot00king/letushavepeaceot00king_djvu.txt, viewed November 1, 2009.
[207] Stirner, quoted in Kingsley 1918.

tears, and the death rattle of the vanquished? Yes, it must."[208]

Otto von Bismarck (1815-1898), in a now-famous 1862 speech: "The great questions of our time will not be settled by resolutions and by majority votes—that was the mistake of 1848 and 1849—but by blood and iron."

Frederick III (1831-1888), German emperor and eighth king of Prussia: "All written Constitutions are scraps of paper."[209]

Otto Von Gottberg (1831-1913), writing in the newspaper *Jungdeutschland-Post* in January 1913: "War is the most august and sacred of human activities." "Let us laugh with all our lungs at the old women in trousers who are afraid of war, and therefore complain that it is cruel and hideous. No! War is beautiful."[210]

Heinrich von Treitschke (1834-1896), an influential professor of history at Humboldt University in Berlin from 1874 to 1896 and member of the Reichstag from 1871, was a rabid nationalist and saw war as Germany's destiny which, guided by a benevolent God, would purge the nation of its sins and make it possible for Germany's superiority to shine forth.

Otto Liebmann (1840-1912), philosopher at the newly-created University of Strassburg after the Franco-Prussian war. Strassburg was intended as a "fortress of the German spirit against France." From the records of the Reichstag debates over the founding of the University of Strassburg:

> "The German universities, resting on the foundation of freedom, are so peculiarly

---

[208] Kuhn, quoted in Kingsley 1918.
[209] Frederick III, quoted in Kingsley 1918.
[210] Gottberg, quoted in Kingsley 1918.

German an institution that no other nation, not even one racially akin, has risen to this institution, and it is for just this reason that a German university is one of the mightiest of all means of again reconciling with the motherland German racial comrades who have long been separated from her ... You may believe, *meine Herren*, that Bonn university has done as much to defend the German Rhineland as have the German fortresses on the Rhein. (Hear hear! On the left)."[211]

Friedrich Nietzsche (1844-1900): "I welcome all signs that a more manly, a warlike, age is about to begin, an age which, above all, will give honor to valor once again. For this age shall prepare the way for one yet higher, and it shall gather the strength which this higher age will need one day—this age which is to carry heroism into the pursuit of knowledge and *wage wars* for the sake of thoughts and their consequences."[212]

Nietzsche: "*War essential.* It is vain rhapsodizing and sentimentality to continue to expect much (even more, to expect a very great deal) from mankind, once it has learned not to wage war. For the time being, we know of no other means to imbue exhausted peoples. as strongly and surely as every great war does, with that raw energy of the battleground, that deep impersonal hatred, that murderous coldbloodedness with a good conscience, that communal, organized ardor in destroying the enemy, that proud indifference to great losses, to one's own existence and to that of one's friends, that muted,

---

[211] Liebmann, quoted in Klaus Christian Köhnke, *The Rise of Neo-Kantianism* (Cambridge University Press, 1991), p. 204.
[212] Nietzsche, *The Gay Science*, § 290.

earthquakelike convulsion of the soul."[213]

Max Lehmann (1845–1929), pastor, political historian, professor at Marburg, Leipzig, and Göttingen, and member of the Prussian Academy: "Germany is the centre of God's plans for the World."[214]

Friedrich von Bernhardi (1849-1930), general, military historian, author of *Germany and the Next War* (1911): "Might is the supreme right," and war is a "divine business," "an indispensable factor of civilization," and "a biological necessity of the first order." And contrasting the French emphasis on rights of liberty and equality, Bernhardi writes of the German philosophy of duty:

> "While the French people in savage revolt against spiritual and secular despotism had broken their chains and proclaimed their *rights*, another quite different revolution was working in Prussia—the revolution of *duty*. The assertion of the rights of the individual leads ultimately to individual irresponsibility and to a repudiation of the State. Immanuel Kant, the founder of critical philosophy, taught, in opposition to this view, the gospel of moral duty, and Scharnhorst grasped the idea of universal military service. By calling upon each individual to sacrifice property and life for the good of the community, he gave the clearest expression to the idea of the State, and created a sound basis on which the claim to individual rights might rest at the same time Stein laid the foundations of self-employed-government in Prussia."[215]

---

[213] Nietzsche, *Human, All-too-Human*, § 477.
[214] Lehmann, quoted in Kingsley 1918.
[215] Bernhardi, *Germany and the Next War* [1911], Chapter 3, http://www.

Houston Stewart Chamberlain (1855-1927), English-born German author and propagandist: "He who does not believe in the Divine Mission of Germany had better go hang himself, and rather today than tomorrow."[216]

Wilhelm II (1859-1941), third German emperor and ninth king of Prussia: "Woe and death to all who shall oppose my will. Woe and death to those who do not believe in my mission."[217]

Otto Richard Tannenberg, author of *Greater Germany, the Work of the Twentieth Century*, writing in 1911: "War must leave nothing to the vanquished but their eyes to weep with."[218]

Ernst Troeltsch (1865-1923), theologian and Neo-Kantian professor of philosophy at Heidelberg: Struggle is a test of a culture's vital forces, in which "the fullness of contending national spirits ... unfold their highest spiritual powers."[219]

Max Scheler (1874-1928), philosopher at the universities of Jena, Munich, and Cologne, writing on the German ideology: "It would set faith against skepticism, metaphysics against science, the organic whole against atomism, life against mechanism, heroism against calculation, true community against commercialized society, a hierarchically ordered people against the mass leveled down by egalitarianism."[220]

---

gutenberg.org/files/11352/11352.txt. Viewed October 15, 2009.

[216] Chamberlain, quoted in Kingsley 1918.

[217] Wilhelm II, quoted in Kingsley 1918.

[218] Tannenberg, quoted in Kingsley 1918.

[219] Troeltsch, quoted in Arthur Herman, *The Idea of Decline* (Free Press, 1997), p. 233.

[220] Scheler, quoted in Helmut Kuhn, "German Philosophy and National Socialism," *The Encyclopedia of Philosophy* (MacMillan, 1963), p. 313.

Thomas Mann (1875-1955), novelist and essayist, echoing the desire to eliminate the old world of bourgeois hypocrisy, thought the war would end that "horrible world, which now no longer is, or no longer will be, after the great storm passed by. Did it not crawl with spiritual vermin as with worms?"[221]

Mann, writing during the war of his pre-war days: "We knew it, this world of peace. We suffered from this horrible world more acutely than anyone else. It stank of the ferments of decomposition. The artist was so sick of this world that he praised God for this purge and this tremendous hope."[222]

Georg Heym (1887-1912), German Expressionist poet, on the eve of World War I:

> "Everything is always the same, so boring, boring, boring. Nothing ever happens, absolutely nothing. ... If someone would only begin a war, it need not be a just one."[223]

> In his diary of 1911: "Most of all I would like to be a lieutenant of the cuirassiers. But the day after I want to be a terrorist." Later that year: "without my Jacobin hat I cannot envisage myself. Now I hope that there will at least be a war."[224]

Ernst Jünger (1895-1998), author of *Storm of Steel*, after returning from World War I, in which he had been wounded three times, on how defeated Germany was by the war:

> We are "a new generation, a race that has been

---

[221] Mann, quoted in Fritz Stern, *The Failure of Illiberalism: Essays on the Political Culture of Modern Germany* (A. A. Knopf, 1972), p. 120.
[222] Mann, quoted in Walter Laqueur, *Weimar: A Cultural History, 1918-1933* (G. P. Putnam's Sons, 1974), pp. 115-116.
[223] Heym, quoted in Herman 1997, p. 235.
[224] Heym, quoted in Laqueur 1974, 115.

hardened and inwardly transformed by all the darting flames and sledgehammer blows of the greatest war in history."[225]

In war, "the true human being makes up in a drunken orgy for everything that he has been neglecting. Then his passions, too long damned up by society and its laws, become once more dominant and holy and the ultimate reason." And again: "This war is not ended, but the chord that heralds new power. It is the anvil on which the world will be hammered into new boundaries and new communities. New forms will be filled with blood, and might will be hammered into them with a hard fist. War is a great school, and the new man will be of our cut."[226]

Describing the warrior's entry into battle: "Now the task is to gather oneself. Yes, perhaps it is a pity. Perhaps as well we are sacrificing ourselves for something inessential. But no on can rob us of *our* value. Essential is not *what* we are fighting for, but *how* we fight. Onward toward the goal, until we triumph or are left behind. The warriors' spirit, the exposure of oneself to risk, even for the tiniest idea, weighs more heavily in the scale than all the brooding about good and evil."[227]

Oswald Spengler (1880-1936), author of *The Decline of the West*: "We must go right through to the end in our misfortune;

---

[225] Jünger, quoted in Herman 1997, p. 243.
[226] Jünger, quoted in Gordon A. Craig, *Germany, 1866-1945* (Oxford University Press, 1978), p. 492.
[227] Jünger, "Feuer" (1922). Excerpted in Anton Kaes, Martin Jay, and Edward Dimendberg, eds. *The Weimar Republic Sourcebook* (University of California Press, 1994), p. 20.

we need a chastisement compared to which the four years of war are nothing. ... A dictatorship, resembling that of Napoleon, will be regarded universally as a salvation. But then blood must flow, the more the better."[228]

Otto Braun, age 19, volunteer who died in World War I, in a letter to his parents: "My inmost yearning, my purest, though most secret flame, my deepest faith and my highest hope— they are still the same as ever, and they all bear one name: the State. One day to build the state like a temple, rising up pure and strong, resting in its own weight, severe and sublime, but also serene like the gods and with bright halls glistening in the dancing brilliance of the sun—this, at bottom, is the end and goal of my aspirations."[229]

Some commentators on Germany in the nineteenth and early twentieth centuries:

R. Kevin Hill, American historian of philosophy: "associations between Kantian duty and military experience became increasingly common in late nineteenth-century Germany, especially after the Schiller and Fichte centennials."[230]

Friedrich Meinecke (1862-1954), German historian, writing in 1950: "The German power-state idea, whose history began with Hegel, was to find in Hitler its worst and most fatal application and extension."[231]

---

[228] Spengler, quoted in Otto Friedrich, *Before the Deluge: A Portrait of Berlin in the 1920's* (Harper & Row, 1972), p. 351.
[229] Braun, quoted in Kuhn 1963, p. 313.
[230] Hill, *Nietzsche's Critiques: the Kantian Foundations of His Thought* (Oxford, 2003), p. 27; see also Köhnke, *NeoKantianism*, pp. 115-24.
[231] Meinecke, *The German Catastrophe*. Translated by Sidney B. Fay (Harvard University Press, 1950), p. 15.

American historian William Manchester on nineteenth-century Germany: "the poetic genius of the youth of Germany was saturated with militaristic ideals, and death in battle was prized as a sacred duty on behalf of Fatherland, home, and family."[232]

Ernst Gläser (1902–1963), German novelist expressing the prevailing spirit of 1914: "At last life had regained an ideal significance. The great virtues of humanity ... fidelity, patriotism, readiness to die for an ideal ... were triumphing over the trading and shopkeeping spirit ... This was the providential lightning flash that would clear the air [and make way for] a new world directed by a race of noble souls who would root out all signs of degeneracy and lead humanity back to the deserted peaks of the eternal ideals ... The war would cleanse mankind from all its impurities."[233]

---

[232] Manchester, *The Arms of Krupp* (Little, Brown, and Co., 1964), p. 63.
[233] Gläser, quoted in Craig 1978, p. 340.

Bibliography

Ahern, Daniel R. 1995. *Nietzsche as Cultural Physician*. Pennsylvania State University Press.

Allison, David B. 2001. *Reading the New Nietzsche*. Rowman and Littlefield.

Anchor, Robert. 1972. *Germany Confronts Modernization, German Culture and Society, 1790-1890*. D. C. Heath.

Barkai, Avraham. 1990. *Nazi Economics: Ideology, Theory, and Policy*. Yale University Press.

Barnard, F. M. 1965. *Herder's Social and Political Thought: From Enlightenment to Nationalism*. Oxford: Clarendon Press.

Bernhardi, Friedrich von. 1911. *Germany and the Next War*. http://www. gutenberg.org/files/11352/11352.txt. Viewed October 15, 2009.

Beck, Lewis White. 1963. "German Philosophy." *The Encyclopedia of Philosophy*. MacMillan.

Berlin, Isaiah. 1980. "The Counter-Enlightenment." *Against the Current*. Viking Press.

Brüggemeier, Franz-Joseph, Marc Cioc, and Thomas Zeller, editors. 2005. *How Green Were the Nazis?* Athens: Ohio University Press.

Burleigh, Michael. 2000. *The Third Reich: A New History*. Hill and Wang.

Cobden, Richard 1903. *Political Writings of Richard Cobden*. Vol. I, 4ᵗʰ ed. London: T. Fisher Unwin.

Cohen, Carl, editor. 1962. *Communism, Fascism, and Democracy: The Theoretical Foundations*. Random House.

Courtois, Stéphane, Werth, Nicolas, Panné, Jean-Louis, Paczkowski, Karel Bartosek, and Margolin, Jean-Louis, editors. *The Black Book of Communism: Crimes, Terror, Repression* [1997]. Translated by Jonathan Murphy and Mark Kramer. Harvard University Press, 1999.

Cowan, Marianne. 1962. "Introduction" to *Philosophy in the Tragic Age of the Greeks*. South Bend, Indiana: Gateway Editions.

Craig, Gordon A. 1978. *Germany, 1866-1945*. Oxford University Press.

Fichte, Johann. 1922 [1806]. *Addresses to the German Nation*. Translated by R. F. Jones and G. H. Turnbull. Open Court.

Friedrich, Otto. 1972. *Before the Deluge: A Portrait of Berlin in the 1920's*. Harper & Row.

Gerhard, Gesine. 2005. "Breeding Pigs and People for the Third Reich: Richard Walther Darré's Agrarian Ideology." In Brüggemeier et al. 2005, 129-146.

Gilman, Sander L., editor. 1987. *Conversations with Nietzsche: A Life in the Words of His Contemporaries*. Translated by David J. Parent. Oxford University Press.

Goebbels, Joseph. 1925. *Michael*. In Mosse, ed., 1966.

Goebbels, Joseph. 1932. "Those Damned Nazis." Pamphlet.

Goebbels, Josef. 1948. *The Goebbels Diaries*. Edited by Louis P. Lochner. New York: Popular Library.

Goldhagen, Daniel Jonah. 1996. *Hitler's Willing Executioners*. A. A. Knopf.

Hayek, Friedrich. 1944. "The Socialist Roots of Naziism." In *The Road to Serfdom*. University of Chicago Press.

Hayman, Ronald. 1980. *Nietzsche: A Critical Life*. Oxford University Press.

Hegel, G. W. F. 1991 [1837]. *The Philosophy of History*. Translated by J. Sibree. Prometheus Books.

Heidegger, Martin. 1982. *Nietzsche*, Vol. 4. Edited by David Krell. Harper and Row.

Heiden, Konrad. 1971. "Introduction" to *Mein Kampf*, Ralph Manheim translation.

Herman, Arthur. 1997. *The Idea of Decline in Western History*. Free Press.

Hill, R. Kevin. 2003. *Nietzsche's Critiques: The Kantian Foundations of His Thought*. Oxford University Press.

Hitler, Adolf. 1971 [1925]. *Mein Kampf*. Translated by Ralph Manheim. Boston: Houghton Mifflin.

Hunt, Lester. 1991. *Nietzsche and the Origin of Virtue*. London and New York: Routledge.

Irving, David. 1999. *Goebbels, Mastermind of the Third Reich*. Focal Point Editions. Web version.

Kaes, Anton, Martin Jay, and Edward Dimendberg, eds. 1994. *The Weimar Republic Sourcebook*. University of California Press.

Kant, Immanuel. 1951 [1790]. *Critique of Judgment*. Translated by J. H. Bernard. Haffner Press.

Kant, Immanuel. 1983 [1786]. "Speculative Beginning of Human History." In *Perpetual Peace and Other Essays*, translated by Ted Humphrey. Indianapolis: Hackett Publishing.

Kater, Michael H. 2004. *Hitler Youth*. Harvard University Press.

Kater, Michael H. 1983. *The Nazi Party: A Social Profile of Members and Leaders, 1919-1945*. Harvard University Press.

Kaufmann, Walter. 1975. *Existentialism from Dostoevsky to Sartre*. New American Library.

Kaufmann, Walter. 1974. *Nietzsche: Philosopher, Psychologist, Antichrist*. Princeton University Press.

Keegan, John. 1999. *The First World War*. A. A. Knopf.

Kingsley, Darwin P. 1918. "Woodrow Wilson and the Doctrine of Sovereignty." *Addresses of the Empire Club of Canada*. Delivered October 17, 1918.

Köhnke, Klaus Christian. 1991. *The Rise of Neo-Kantianism*. Cambridge University Press.

Koonz, Claudia. 2003. *The Nazi Conscience*. Belknap Press of Harvard University Press. See especially Chapter 2, "The Politics of Virtue," and Chapter 3, "Allies in the Academy."

Kuhn, Helmut. 1963. "German Philosophy and National Socialism." *The Encyclopedia of Philosophy*. MacMillan/Free Press, pp. 309-316.

Lampert, Laurence. 1986. *Nietzsche's Teaching*. New Haven: Yale University Press.

Langer, Walter C. 1944. *A Psychological Analysis of Adolph Hitler His Life and Legend*. Office of Strategic Services, Washington, D.C. http://www.ess. uwe.ac.uk/documents/osstitle.htm. Viewed July 22, 2005.

Laqueur, Walter. 1974. *Weimar: A Cultural History, 1918-1933*. G. P. Putnam's Sons.

Lauryssens, Stan. 1999. *The Man Who Invented the Third Reich*. Sutton.

Lefkowitz, Eliott. 2006. "The Holocaust." http://www.spertus.edu/learnmore/ holocaust.php. Viewed February 18, 2006.

Leiter, Brian. 2004. "Nietzsche's Moral and Political Philosophy." http://plato. stanford.edu/entries/nietzsche-moral-political/. Viewed September 4, 2008.

Leiter, Brian. 2001. "The Paradox of Fatalism and Self-Creation." In Richardson and Leiter.

Lifton, Robert Jay. 1986. *The Nazi Doctors: Medical Killing and the Psychology of Genocide*. Basic Books.

Lilla, Mark. 1997. "The Enemy of Liberalism." *New York Review of Books*, May 15.

Lukacs, John. 1991. *The Duel, 10 May - 31 July 1940, The Eighty-day Struggle Between Churchill and Hitler*. New York: Ticknor and Fields.

Mack, Michael. 2003. *German Idealism and the Jew*. Chicago: University of Chicago Press.

Magnus, Bernd and Higgins, Kathleen, editors. 1996. *The Cambridge Companion to Nietzsche*. Cambridge University Press.

Manchester, William. 1964. *The Arms of Krupp*. Little, Brown, and Co., 1964.

Manchester, William. 1989. *The Last Lion, Winston Spencer Churchill, Alone, 1932-1940*. Delta.

Meinecke, Friedrich. 1950. *The German Catastrophe*. Translated by Sidney B. Fay. Harvard University Press.

Meinecke, Friedrich. 1977. *The Age of German Liberation, 1795-1815*. U. of California Press.

Mill, John Stuart. 1909 [1848]. *Principles of Political Economy with some of their Applications to Social Philosophy*. Edited by William J. Ashley. http://www.econlib.org/library. Viewed September 1, 2007.

Mises, Ludwig von. 1981 [1922]. *Socialism*. Indianapolis: Liberty Classics.

Mosse, George L., editor. 1966. *Nazi Culture: Intellectual, Cultural and Social Life in the Third Reich*. New York: Grosset and Dunlap.

Murphy, John Patrick Michael. 1999. "Hitler Was *Not* an Atheist." *Free Inquiry* 19:2 (Spring).

Mussolini, Benito. 1963. "The Doctrine of Fascism." In John Somerville and Ronald Santoni, eds., *Social and Political Philosophy, Readings from Plato to Gandhi*. Doubleday/Anchor.

Nietzsche, Friedrich. 2005. *The Anti-Christ, Ecce Homo, Twilight of the Idols, and Other Writings*. Edited by Aaron Ridley. Translated by Judith Norman. Cambridge University Press. [Includes *The Case of Wagner* and *Nietzsche contra Wagner*.]

Nietzsche, Friedrich. 1968. *Basic Writings of Nietzsche*. Edited and translated by Walter Kaufmann. Modern Library.

Nietzsche, Friedrich. 1966 [1886]. *Beyond Good and Evil*. Translated by Walter Kaufmann. New York: Vintage.

Nietzsche, Friedrich. 1872. *The Birth of Tragedy*. Translated by Walter Kaufmann. Random.

Nietzsche, Friedrich. 1997. *Daybreak*. Translated by R. J. Hollingdale. Edited by Maudemarie Claude and Brian Leiter. Cambridge University Press.

Stephen Hicks § 149

Nietzsche, Friedrich. 2001 [1882]. *The Gay Science*. Translated by Josefine Nauckhoff and Adrian Del Caro. Cambridge: Cambridge University Press.

Nietzsche, Friedrich. 1996 [1878]. *Human, All Too Human*. Translated by R. J. Hollingdale. Cambridge University Press.

Nietzsche, Friedrich. 1968 [1987]. *On the Genealogy of Morals*. In *Basic Writings of Nietzsche*, edited and translated by Walter Kaufmann. New York: Modern Library.

Nietzsche, Friedrich. 1962. *Philosophy in the Tragic Age of the Greeks*. Translated by Marianne Cowan. South Bend, Indiana: Gateway Editions.

Nietzsche, Friedrich. 1976. *The Portable Nietzsche*. Edited and Translated by Walter Kaufmann. Penguin.

Nietzsche, Friedrich. 1996. *Selected Letters of Friedrich Nietzsche*. Edited and translated by Christopher Middleton. Hackett.

Nietzsche, Friedrich. 1968 [1883-85]. *Thus Spoke Zarathustra*. In *The Portable Nietzsche*, edited and translated by Walter Kaufmann. Penguin.

Nietzsche, Friedrich. 1968. *Twilight of the Idols* and *The Anti-Christ*. Translated by R. J. Hollingdale. Penguin.

Nietzsche, Friedrich. 1997. *Untimely Meditations*, Second edition. Translated and edited by Daniel Breazeale, and R. J. Hollingdale. Cambridge University Press.

Nietzsche, Friedrich. 1957. *The Use and Abuse of History*. Second, revised edition, translated by Adrian Collins. Bobbs-Merrill.

Nietzsche, Friedrich. 1976 [1880]. *The Wanderer and His Shadow*. In *The Portable Nietzsche*, edited and translated by Walter Kaufmann. New York: Penguin.

Nietzsche, Friedrich. 1968. *The Will to Power*. Edited by Walter Kaufmann and translated by Walter Kaufmann and R. J. Hollingdale. Vintage.

Nietzsche, Friedrich. 2003. *Writings from the Late Notebooks*. Translated and edited by Kate Sturge and Rüdiger Bittner. Cambridge University Press.

Nipperdey, Thomas. 1996. *Germany from Napoleon to Bismarck, 1800-1866*. Translated by Daniel Nolan. Princeton University Press.

Orlow, Dietrich. 1969. *The History of the Nazi Party, 1919-1933*. University of Pittsburgh Press.

Peikoff, Leonard. 1982. *The Ominous Parallels*. Stein and Day.

Pipes, Richard. 1999. *Property and Freedom*. A. A. Knopf.

Reuth, Ralf Georg. 1990. *Goebbels* (trans. Krishna Winston). New York: Harcourt, Brace, and Co.

Richardson, John, and Leiter, Brian, editors. 2001. *Nietzsche*. Oxford Readings in Philosophy. Oxford University Press.

Rohkrämer, Thomas. 2005. "Martin Heidegger, National Socialism, and Environmentalism." In Brüggemeier et al. 2005, 171-203.

Rosen, Stanley. 1995. *The Mask of Enlightenment: Nietzsche's* Zarathustra. Cambridge University Press.

Rummel, R. J. 1997. *Death by Government*. Transaction Publishers.

Shirer, William L. 1962. *The Rise and Fall of the Third Reich*. Greenwich CT: Crest.

Shorris, Earl. 2007. *The Politics of Heaven: America in Fearful Times*. New York: W.W. Norton & Co.

Solomon, Robert. 2003. *Living with Nietzsche*. Oxford University Press.

Stern, Fritz. 1972. *The Failure of Illiberalism: Essays on the Political Culture of Modern Germany*. A. A. Knopf.

Taylor, A. J. P. 1945. *The Course of German History, A Survey of the Development of Germany Since 1815*. Hamish Hamilton.

Taylor, A. J. P. 1995. *From Napoleon to the Second International*. Penguin.

Toland, John. 1976. *Adolf Hitler: The Definitive Biography*. Anchor.

Weinreich, Max. 1999. *Hitler's Professors*. Yale University Press.

Weiss, John. 1996. *Ideology of Death: Why the Holocaust Happened in Germany*. Ivan Dee Publishers.

Winds of Change. 2005. "Mein Kampf a Bestseller in Turkey." http://www.windsofchange.net/archives/006690.php. Post published April 20, 2005. Viewed June 30, 2006 and August 24, 2009.

Index

Image Credits

Austrian Armed Forces

Charles E. Snyder, Jr., Major, USAF (Retired), Snyder's
Treasures Website

Douglas Anderson, Associate Professor, Concordia College

Randall Bytwerk, Calvin College

Chris Merwe, "The King," Creative Commons Attribtion
license

Christopher Vaughan, "Hitler and Nietzsche"

Goethe-Schiller Archive, Weimar

Acknowledgments

Rockford College provided a research grant that enabled the writing of the first draft of the script. Virginia Murr researched the Nazi eugenics movement and proofread the manuscript. Quee Nelson shared several new-to-me quotations from key figures in the National Socialist movement. Anja Hartleb-Parson provided valuable editing and reference checking. Kira Newman proofread the index. And Christopher Vaughan designed the book edition.

Made in the USA
Middletown, DE
13 May 2024

54304937R00102